Developing a Leadership Training Model for Churches

A Biblical Perspective

Endale Gebremeskel Ousman

ACADEMIC

© 2024 Endale Gebremeskel Ousman

Published 2024 by Langham Academic
An imprint of Langham Publishing
www.langhampublishing.org

Langham Publishing and its imprints are a ministry of Langham Partnership

Langham Partnership
PO Box 296, Carlisle, Cumbria, CA3 9WZ, UK
www.langham.org

ISBNs:
978-1-78641-001-6 Print
978-1-78641-097-9 ePub
978-1-78641-098-6 PDF

Endale Gebremeskel Ousman has asserted his right under the Copyright, Designs and Patents Act, 1988 to be identified as the Author of this work.

All rights reserved. No part of this publication may be reproduced, stored in a retrieval system or transmitted, in any form or by any means, electronic, mechanical, photocopying, recording or otherwise, without the prior written permission of the publisher or the Copyright Licensing Agency.

Requests to reuse content from Langham Publishing are processed through PLSclear. Please visit www.plsclear.com to complete your request.

Scriptures taken from the Holy Bible, New International Version®, NIV®. Copyright © 1973, 1978, 1984, 2011 by Biblica, Inc.™ Used by permission of Zondervan.

British Library Cataloguing-in-Publication Data
A catalogue record for this book is available from the British Library

ISBN: 978-1-78641-001-6

Cover & Book Design: projectluz.com

Langham Partnership actively supports theological dialogue and an author's right to publish but does not necessarily endorse the views and opinions set forth here or in works referenced within this publication, nor can we guarantee technical and grammatical correctness. Langham Partnership does not accept any responsibility or liability to persons or property as a consequence of the reading, use or interpretation of its published content.

Developing a Leadership Training Model for Churches: A Biblical Perspective is an exceptional resource for any church leader in Africa looking to enrich their knowledge and practical application for church planting and growth, as well as leadership. The detail in this book provides much insight and wisdom.

Daniel Belay
Pastor,
Eritrean Bethel Church London, UK

The church in Africa continues to grapple with the critical need for theological education and pastoral leadership development. Key challenges include relevance of curricula, accessibility, affordability, and learning or teaching methodologies. In a quest for an alternative model of training, Dr. Endale G. Ousman's work, *Developing a Leadership Training Model for Churches: A Biblical Perspective*, makes a sterling contribution for contextualized model(s) of pastoral leadership development in the church in Africa.

Many existing theological institutions were designed and established by Western missionaries and successive national leaderships have often sought to maintain and preserve Western models and teaching methodologies. Ousman proposes a reformation and expansion of existing programs and more importantly, innovative ways of overcoming the challenges for effective theological and leadership development in the church. This work is timely, and highly commended for theological educators and leadership development.

Aiah Foday-Khabenje, DMin, PhD
Former General Secretary,
Association of Evangelicals in Africa (AEA), Kenya

Endale Gebremeskel Ousman has authored an essential book that equips emerging leaders with a holistic perspective, crucially avoiding a "dichotomous view of overemphasizing spiritual needs and neglecting the holistic needs of society." His extensive experience with local and national churches, along with his teaching in Bible colleges, led him to develop a Bible-based, Jesus-modelled, church-owned, and community-oriented training program within the Ethiopian church.

Ousman's profound passion for comprehensive leadership training is truly inspiring. As one of his mentees, I am deeply influenced by his life and ministry.

This book pierces to the heart of what makes a leadership training model truly effective and accessible within the church, serving as a vital resource for its future.

Endalkachew Tefera
Lead Pastor,
Ethiopian Fellowship Church, North Carolina, USA

Contents

Abstract ix
    Developing a Leadership Training Model for Churches:
      A Biblical Perspective

Acknowledgments xi

Chapter 1 1
    The Problem
      Introduction 1
      Purpose 5
      Research Questions 5
      Definition of Terms 6
      Ministry Project 6
      Context 7
      Overview 8

Chapter 2 9
    Literature
      Introduction 9
      Description of the Dissertation Project 10
      Biblical/Theological Foundation 10
      The Training Experience of the Church in the Past 16
      Theological Doctrines Relevant to Alternative Leadership
          Training Models That Are Culturally Contextualized 18
      Alternative Leadership Training That Is Culturally Contextualized 26
      History of Theological Education in Ethiopia 27
      Theological Education/Leadership Training Model(s) in
          Ethiopia Compared with Model(s) in Other Regions of the
          World 29
      Research Design 40
      Summary 41

Chapter 3 43
    Methodology
      Research Questions 43
      Population and Participants 45
      Design of the Study 47
      Data Collection 57
      Data Analysis 63
      Ethical Procedures 63

Chapter 4 67
   Findings
      Participants 67
      Research Question #1 69
      Research Question #2 83
      Research Question #3 88
      Summary of Major Findings 95

Chapter 5 97
   Discussion
      Major Findings 97
      Implications of the Findings 115
      Limitations of the Study 121
      Unexpected Observations 123
      Recommendations 124
      Postscript 126

Appendix A 133
   Summary of the Population of People Groups Represented by the Cultural Focus Groups of the Hiwot Berhan Church

Appendix B 135
   Components of Expert Review

Appendix C 137
   Interview Protocol for Focus Groups

Appendix D 139
   Interview Protocol for Individuals

Appendix E 141
   Curriculum for Loke Bible School

Appendix F 143
   Curriculum for Pentecostal Theological College

Appendix G 149
   Curriculum for Adola Bible School

Appendix H 151
   Curriculum for Worancha Bible School

Appendix I 153
   Ways in Which Churches Can Partner to Make Leadership Training Programs Culturally Relevant and Financially Sustainable

Bibliography 159

List of Tables

Table 2.1 Summary of the Literature Review 39

Table 3.1 Participants of the Focus Groups 46

Table 3.2 The Region and Number of Participants in the Individual Interviews 47

Table 4.1 Participants and Demographics 68

Table 4.2 Participants' Responses on the Spiritual Qualities of an Ideal Church Leader in the Context of the Hiwot Berhan Church 71

Table 4.3 Participants' Responses on the Cultural Qualities of an Ideal Church Leader in the Context of the Hiwot Berhan Church 72

Table 4.4 Participants' Responses as to the Effectiveness of Formal Theological Training 74

Table 4.5 Types of Alternative Church Leadership Training Recommended by Focus Groups 78

Table 4.6 Types of Alternative Church Leadership Training and the Delivery Systems Recommended by Individual Interviewees 80

Table 4.7 Characteristics Unique to Each Region 82

Table 4.8 Social and Cultural Values That Are Threats to Leadership Development and the Biblical Christian Values Recommended by Participants 86

Table 4.9 A Comparison between the Existing Curricula and the Recommended Biblical Christian Values 89

Table 4.10 The Availability of the Scriptures in the Languages of the Participants 91

Table 4.11 Population Five Years Old and Above by Literacy, 2007 92

Table 5.1 Types of Skilled Workers in the Tabernacle 105

Table 5.2 Basic Leadership Training 117

Table 5.3 Advanced Leadership Training 118

Abstract

Developing a Leadership Training Model for Churches: A Biblical Perspective

This research was conducted in the Hiwot Berhan Church of Ethiopia, one of the largest evangelical/Pentecostal denominations in the country. Pentecostal missionaries from Sweden pioneered the church in 1960. Both the mission and the church have been conducting short-term leadership training and residential Bible schools since their early days. However, these programs have not been based on an assessment of the needs of the churches. Therefore, I conducted this research among the Hiwot Berhan churches with the purpose of exploring the essential elements of an alternative leadership training program that is culturally contextualized.

The findings in this research indicated five essential elements needed for effective church leadership training programs in the Hiwot Berhan Church. First, identifying the ideal church leader in the contexts of the Hiwot Berhan churches was foundational for training. Second, the curricula for the formal theological institutes need to be revised and reformed because their limitations outweigh their contributions. Third, the churches require newer types of alternative leadership training programs that are more accessible and affordable. Fourth, the curricula for these alternative leadership programs need to include community leadership values as well as relevant biblical values that are recommended by the leadership of the Hiwot Berhan churches. Fifth, the ability of these leadership training programs to be financially self-supporting needs to be ensured by the leadership of the Hiwot Berhan churches so that the programs become sustainable over the long term.

Acknowledgments

I give all the glory and praise to God, the Father of our Lord Jesus Christ, for enabling me to accomplish this academic phase of my purpose in life. I would like to thank my dear wife, Fantaye Alemu Lalego, who is my partner in life and in the ministry, for her love, prayer, support, and perseverance. I also thank our dear children, Sibhat, Yelayou and his wife Alsemu, Tamiru, Meron, and Beza, who have always been a source of joy and comfort in my spiritual pilgrimage. I want to express my gratitude to Dr. Thomas Tumblin, the dean of the Beeson International Center, for his mentorship during the process of my research writing. I am greatly indebted to the Beeson International Center for their provision, support, and hospitality. Dr. Frew Tamirat, the principal of the Evangelical Theological College in Ethiopia, has been a continuous source of motivation in this academic journey. The leadership of the Ethiopian Hiwot Berhan Church has cooperated with me fully in the process of the research. The Swedish Pentecostal Church has supported me financially toward the logistics the research process required. I wish you all the Lord's blessings. I also want to express my appreciation to the editors, the Research Reflection Team members, and the external auditors, whose professional input has enriched my research.

CHAPTER 1

The Problem

Introduction

In 1973, I began full-time ministry as a student and interpreter in a certificate-level Bible school in Hawassa, Ethiopia. After finishing the certificate program, I was assigned to work as an assistant to Swedish missionaries. Since that time, my work has involved training Ethiopian Christian leaders both in a Bible school and in a church setting. Furthermore, I have worked with degree-granting theological colleges during the last twenty years both as a teacher and as an administrator. While undertaking this work I first felt a burden for developing an alternative leadership training model that is culturally contextualized for church leaders in Ethiopia.

According to the statistical country-level report by the 2007 Population and Housing Census of Ethiopia, the total population of Ethiopia was 73,750,932. Of this number, about 80 percent lives in rural areas where agriculture and pastoralism constitute their livelihoods.[1] In addition, this population information implies that the majority of the evangelical churches and Christian ministers are located in rural areas where the literacy rate is very low.[2]

Missionary Melvin L. Hodges identifies leadership development as the missing link in the missionary task in Latin America. Hodges writes, "In this case, we are at least partially training them *away* from the task instead of *for*

---

1. Woldesemait, "Some Thoughts," 21–47.
2. Woldesemait, 38.

the task."³ Hodges lists four training gaps: first, a gap between the intellectual development and the spiritual development of the worker; second, a gap between knowledge and practical ministry; third, a wide gap between the clergy and the laity; and fourth, a serious gap in the concept of the role that the training of workers plays in the development of the church.⁴

Although Hodges's material was first written in 1953 evangelical churches and theological institutions in Ethiopia share these same gaps equally. The problems in church leadership training include the following. First, the curricula in most Ethiopian theological institutions of higher education were initially designed either by Western missionaries who pioneered the work or by nationals who duplicated Western models of theological institutions. Second, the curricula in many of the theological programs in formal higher education institutions have served for so long that they seem untouchable even after institutional leadership has been transferred to nationals. Third, while the biblical studies divisions of these curricula are still applicable, the ministerial and theological courses lack relevancy from a cultural and practical perspective. Fourth, most of the theological institutions are located in urban centers at a distance not easily accessible for rural church leaders. Fifth, most rural church ministers cannot fulfill the academic entrance requirements required by the formal theological institutions. Sixth, the theological programs in formal higher education institutions also face a problem of duplication of program types, course contents, and teaching methodologies. Often the programs lack originality and program specification based on churches' training needs, and very few of the programs have departments or areas focusing on Christian leadership.⁵ Seventh, most of the formal theological institutions are designed for full-time, vocational church leaders who are able to spend two to four years in residence as part of the program. As such, these programs often do not suit the available workers in the Ethiopian evangelical church setting.⁶ Eighth, in light of the monthly income of an average evangelical minister, and also of the average annual budget of a rural church in Ethiopia, the training costs associated with formal theological institutions prove unaffordable to

---

3. Hodges, *Indigenous Church*, 55.
4. Hodges, 58–59.
5. Yilma, "Impact Assessment," 49–51.
6. Bellete, *Agonies and Hallelujahs*, 340–41.

many churches and church leaders.[7] Ninth, in a country where poverty, social injustice, violations of women's and children's rights, and other social and economic problems are prevalent, most of the curricula in the theological institutions lack a holistic perspective and approach.[8] Instead, these programs are still dominated by a dichotomous view, which overemphasizes spiritual needs and neglects the holistic needs of the society.

Wondaferaw A. Ersulo lists some of the negative outcomes of formal theological trainings in Ethiopia. First, the graduates become arrogant, critical about the church and its leadership, and divisive in churches by seeking power. Second, they show fewer good qualities such as grace and humility. Third, training centers have become places in which trainees lose the spiritual values and practices they previously had. Fourth, the curricula focus more on developing intellectual capacity and less on spiritual formation and integration. Fifth, the content and method of training in leadership training centers are among the causes of conflict between established church leaders and young ministers graduating from training centers.[9]

Elie A. Buconyori defines Christian education thus: "Education is the interpersonal process of learning to become [a] Christ like and self-reliant person in society."[10] The writer is referring to the educational task of the church in schools, in higher education, and in the church itself. This definition proposes four components of a quality Christian education: an interpersonal component, Christlikeness, self-reliance, and a societal component – and these imply the type of theological education required in Ethiopia.

The foundation for this research was my conviction that a training program for church leadership in Ethiopia must be Bible based, Jesus modeled, church owned, and community oriented. Buconyori lists five components of Christian education in the early church. These components imply that education in the early church was scriptural, Christ centered, and church owned.[11] Although individuals often initiate ministry visions, a vision for alternative leadership training models that are culturally contextualized must ultimately

---

7. Ararso, *Biblical Principles*, 207.
8. Balisky, "Contemporary Theological Perspective," 57.
9. Ersulo, "Bridging the Gap," 187–89.
10. Buconiyori, *Educational Task*, 40.
11. Buconiyori, 40.

be owned and implemented by the churches that select, appoint, sponsor, and commission the trainees. I began to understand the need for these alternative leadership training models through my ministerial observation and active participation in leadership training programs both in Bible school and in church settings. The resources for such information were vocational and bivocational leaders of evangelical churches (those leaders in the Hiwot Berhan and sister evangelical churches) and students in my classes at different theological colleges where I spent the last twenty years of my ministry.

The congregants of evangelical churches proved the best sources to assess leadership training needs. I have spent years among churches of diverse creeds and confessions listening to congregants' appreciation of, complaints against, and desires for their church leaders. I have taught and mentored hundreds of students in my classes at five theological institutions of higher education in the country. The students came from various theological and cultural backgrounds. Their written assignments and the interactions I had with them in class, outside class, and at their churches whenever they invited me to preach provided additional sources that inspired me to focus on developing a culturally relevant, contemporary, and accessible alternative training program for church leaders at the grassroots level.

My rationale for this project included several core values. First, alternative training models that are culturally contextualized for church leaders should be designed on the basis and practice of biblical models of training with special emphasis on Jesus's model of training the twelve disciples. Concerning Jesus's example in ministry, Robert E. Coleman writes, "Of those things which are carefully selected and recorded in absolute integrity under the inspiration of the Holy Spirit, we can be sure that they are intended to teach us how to follow in the way of the Master."[12] Coleman describes the life and work of Jesus recorded in the gospels as a *textbook on evangelism* as well as every area of God's mission. Günter Krallmann summarizes Jesus's contribution to leadership training thus: "Jesus' training of the Twelve established once and for all the consummated normative paradigm for Christian leadership development."[13] Second, I recommend church-based alternative leadership training models. Accordingly, the church both as the body of Christ and as

---

12. Coleman, *Master Plan*, 22.
13. Kralllmann, *Mentoring for Mission*, 14.

a local congregation owns and operates the training program of its leaders. This ownership should include the daily operation of the training program or full partnership in a church leadership training program. Third, I propose community-based alternative leadership training models by integrating the spiritual, social, cultural, and economic needs of the society among which the church exists and operates.

Fourth, these alternative leadership training models are productive if they are needs based, culturally relevant, cost effective, accessible to most churches, and use the trainees' language as a medium of instruction. Fifth, alternative leadership training models are required to have curriculum, teaching materials, teachers, and modes of instruction all aligned to the researched needs of the participants.[14] Finally, these programs also need to be financially self-supporting and sustainable.[15]

Purpose

The purpose of this research was to propose alternative leadership training models that are culturally contextualized for evangelical church leaders in Ethiopia by exploring the training elements needed for potential content and means of delivery through focus group interviewing, semistructured individual interviews, gathering documents, and observations from the Hiwot Berhan Church of Ethiopia within a period of six months.

Research Questions

I applied the following three research questions together with their subquestions to gather the necessary data from the individuals who participated both in the focus group and in one-on-one interviews.

Research Question #1

What are the alternative leadership training elements needed by the Hiwot Berhan Church of Ethiopia at the local, regional, and national levels?

---

14. Buconyori, *Educational Task*, 72.
15. Hodges, *Indigenous Church*, 74–90.

Research Question #2

How can these alternative leadership training elements be grounded in evangelical scriptural knowledge?

Research Question #3

How can a church leadership training program be culturally relevant and economically sustainable in order to meet the long-term leadership needs of the church?

Definition of Terms

A clear definition of the concept of "cultural contextualization" is necessary in order to understand this ministry project. Krallmann defines contextualization in relation to training thus: "Contextualization relative to leadership training implies the content in question is communicated in a culturally viable manner, is shared with nationals on their terms, and is clothed in an indigenous garb."[16] Based on this definition, alternative leadership training models that are culturally contextualized include at least two key components. First, they are Bible based, Jesus modeled, church owned, and community oriented. Second, this type of leadership training program utilizes a specific process and practice of designing a curriculum, recruiting teachers, selecting teaching methods, and allocating resources for leadership training programs in the context of the community.

The term "vocational leaders" in this research refers to the full-time ordained ministers of the church. The term "bivocational leaders" refers to faithful lay leaders, such as church elders and deacons in the context of Ethiopian evangelical churches, who have their own professions yet have committed themselves to the leadership ministry of the church.

Ministry Project

The reader will find the problem addressed in this project discussed in detail in chapter 3, the Methodology section.[17]

---

16. Krallmann, *Mentoring for Mission*, 166.
17. The problem discussed in this research is cited in chapter 3, Methodology

I made the following preparations for this ministry project. Initially I secured verbal and written support from the Hiwot Berhan Church of Ethiopia. For the next step, I established the Research Reflection Team (RRT). I then designed the interview questions in consultation with the RRT.

Right after the approval of the proposal for the ministry project, the following steps were taken to enhance the collection of data. First, I conducted an interview with a pilot focus group to test the relevancy and clarity of the interview questions. Then I arranged the setting for video recording and photographing. Third, I asked for and received permission from the participants and institutions. Fourth, I gave written handouts and a verbal briefing to the participants in the focus groups concerning the benefits they could expect from the research outcomes and the ethical responsibilities required from both parties in the process of the project implementation. Fifth, I conducted individual and focus group interviews in the different settings within the given time frame. I performed the collection of documents and observation simultaneously with the interviews. Sixth, I gathered the data from the individual interviews, focus group interviews, documentation, and observation. Finally, I recorded, analyzed, and organized the data in preparation for reporting. I then reported my findings to the dissertation committee.

I interviewed a total of thirty participants, and all were interviewed in the official language, Amharic, while sometimes being assisted with their vernacular. I used translators and interpreters during the interview process and at the time of transcription. I used laptop computers, video cameras, and audio recorders for the collection of data from the participants. My denominational office covered the transport and per diem expenses of the participants and the translation team.

Context

I conducted this ministry project within the local context of the Hiwot Berhan Church of Ethiopia. In addition, I included four subcontexts within the wider national context, which were the Sidama regional churches, the Oromo-Guji regional churches, the Amhara regional churches, and churches from southwestern Ethiopia (i.e. Wolayita, Gamo Gofa, Nyangatom, and Tsamai).

The methodology for this project is discussed in chapter 3. The reader will find the details under the Methodology section.[18]

The reader will find the theological framework for this project in chapter 2, the Literature Review section.[19]

Overview

The next four chapters provide a detailed account of how the ministry project was implemented and accomplished. Chapter 2 gives an overview of the related research and literature on the subject of alternative leadership training that is culturally contextualized. Chapter 3 details the design of the project, including the research method, the ministry context and participants involved, the evaluation instrumentation, procedures for data collection, and analysis of the collected data. Chapter 4 reports the findings of the project. Chapter 5 integrates the literature review with the findings of the project. It also presents a summary of the project results, conclusions, and reflections for application in this area of ministry, specifically in the Ethiopian context.

---

18. Methodoly is discussed in detail in chapter 3.
19. Theological Framework is discussed in detail under the Literature Review section.

CHAPTER 2

Literature

Introduction

The Hiwot Berhan Church and its sister evangelical churches operate among diverse ethnic groups in Ethiopia most of whom live in rural areas. The Hiwot Berhan Church and the other evangelical churches in Ethiopia own and operate few theological institutions in light of the vast need for discipleship and leadership development. Buconyori makes the following conclusion about the theological situation in Africa: "Those institutions are still small in numbers and more are being planned."[1] The few theological institutions that exist in Ethiopia are designed on Western models of training and utilize English as the medium of instruction, a language foreign to the learners. As a result, the academic entrance requirements prove difficult for ministers from rural backgrounds.

Therefore, sustainable and alternative leadership training models that are culturally contextualized is a pressing contemporary need in Ethiopia. To that end, I hoped to develop such an alternative leadership training by exploring the needed content and means of delivery by interviewing focus groups from the Hiwot Berhan Church of Ethiopia.

---

1. Buconyori, *Educational Task*, 128.

Description of the Dissertation Project

This dissertation presents discussion regarding the manner in which the existing theological training programs of evangelical institutions in Ethiopia, including those of the Hiwot Berhan Church, are not accessible to the majority of Christian ministers for the reasons mentioned earlier. Determining the need for alternative church leadership training programs, identifying specific components for such training, assessing the relevant methods of delivery, and discovering the resources domestically available are therefore critical.

The following discussion is on the topics of biblical, systematic, and historical theology in order to support the need for such alternative leadership training in Ethiopia.

Biblical/Theological Foundation

This section analyzes the biblical and theological foundations for developing specialized training models for evangelical churches in Ethiopia with a primary focus on the Hiwot Berhan Church of Ethiopia.

Jesus's Example

Jesus's model of training the apostles has served as a timeless example and principle for leadership training for churches throughout the ages.[2] Accordingly, Jesus's model stands as a guiding principle for selecting, training, empowering, and commissioning trainees in contemporary churches.

I chose Mark 3:13–19 as the focal passage to illustrate Jesus's model of training the twelve apostles.[3] Three of the gospel writers record the call and appointment of the apostles: Matthew (10:1–4), Mark (3:13–19), and Luke (6:12–16). However, only Mark states clearly Jesus's purpose in the calling and appointment of his twelve disciples (3:14–15). Mark 3:13–19 stands as an independent pericope, serving as a transition from Jesus's popular ministry to the crowd and their acceptance (1:12 – 3:12), to his challenges from the teachers of the law and his own family members (3:20 – 6:6).[4]

---

2. Krallmann, *Mentoring for Mission*, 14.
3. Badajide Cole, "Mark," in *Africa Bible Commentary*, 1203.
4. Guelich, *Mark 1–8*, 155.

Exegetical Study of Mark 3:13–19

The structure of the passage implies three major units, with each major unit having minor units. Robert A. Guelich describes the passage thus:

> Structurally, the section opens with Jesus calling those he wants and their response (3:13). Then he appoints the twelve apostles for two purposes, to be with him and to be sent in mission with two tasks (3:14–15). Finally the section concludes with a listing of the appointed Twelve. Taken together, we have a story of the calling and appointment of the twelve apostles with 3:14–15 serving as the pivot for the account.[5]

In the first of the three major units in this text, Mark writes about Jesus's calling and appointment of the apostles. In this unit Mark discusses the steps Jesus used when calling the twelve disciples (v. 13a) and the response of the twelve to Jesus's calling (v. 13b). In unit two, the writer identifies the two purposes for which Jesus called his disciples (vv. 14–15): "that they might be with him and that he might send them out to preach and to have authority to drive out demons." The third unit lists the names of the twelve apostles (vv. 16–19).

As Guelich suggested, verses 14 and 15 are key verses around which the intent of the author revolves. The three major units answer the following interpretive questions:

1. What does the group "the twelve" represent?
2. Why did Jesus call and appoint the twelve?
3. Who are the twelve as individuals?

Jesus's Calling and Appointment of the Twelve Apostles (Mark 3:13)

The first major unit answers the first interpretive question related to the multidimensional meaning of "the twelve." Mark writes, "Jesus went up on a mountainside and called to him those he wanted, and they came to him. He appointed twelve – designating them apostles" (3:13a–14a, margin). The text implies the following points about the appointment of the twelve apostles: first, Jesus sought guidance in prayer; second, he exercised sovereign choice of the twelve apostles both as individuals and as a group; third, the twelve

---

5. Guelich, 155.

apostles had individual and collective responses to Jesus's calling; fourth, the twelve apostles symbolically represented the twelve tribes of Israel; and fifth, the twelve apostles realized the purpose of their calling and appointment.

Mark 3:13 states, "Jesus . . . called to him those he wanted." This suggests that Jesus selected the twelve from among other disciples. Stephen Short comments: "Of the crowds who were flocking to Him, Jesus selected twelve men to be constantly with Him, so that they might receive from Him a more intensive spiritual training, and later (6:7; 16:15) be dispatched by Him to preach and heal."[6] Therefore, the twelve apostles were a distinct group selected from among Jesus's followers to be appointed for the specific task of apostleship.

Jesus's selection and appointment of the twelve apostles is an example of how Jesus sought divine guidance on critical occasions.[7] Jesus chose a mountainside for this specific task of selecting his disciples. Several reasons seem to attribute theological significance to Jesus's going up a mountainside. First, the parallel passage in Luke 6:13–16 clearly asserts that Jesus went up on the mountainside to pray. Second, Jesus had a habit of going to a place of solitude for prayer before the events of the day (Mark 1:35). Third, Jesus's mission and priority always involved seeking to fulfill the will of his heavenly Father (John 4:34).

Jesus's selection of the apostles was a sovereign choice. Mark states, "Jesus . . . called to him those he wanted" (3:13a). James R. Edwards writes: "In Jewish religion the disciples chose their rabbi. In Jesus' case, he chose his disciples. Jesus is the sole and exclusive subject of the call. . . . Unlike a rabbi, Jesus is not a means to an ulterior good but is himself the final good."[8]

The principle of sovereign choice is illustrated in the rest of the New Testament at times of leadership selection and appointment (Acts 13:1–3; 20:28). Therefore, the appointment of workers for his work is God's sovereign choice.

Mark records the apostles' response to Jesus's call in simple words. He writes, "And they came to him" (3:13b). Jesus called the twelve disciples prior to this occasion, and they responded individually to the call (1:16–20; 2:14–16). Jesus's call was for a lifetime commitment. Therefore, the apostles'

---

6. Short, "Mark," in *The International Bible Commentary*, 1160.
7. Kapolyo, "Matthew," in *Africa Bible Commentary*, 1177.
8. Edwards, *Mark*, quoted in Stein, *Mark*, 169.

response to come to Jesus was a decision beyond a physical move. Rather, it suggested a lifetime commitment to follow and serve Jesus.[9]

The twelve apostles also have symbolic representation in addition to their own specific tasks.[10] Other passages in the New Testament indicate that the number twelve represents the twelve tribes of Israel (Matt 19:28; Rev 21:12–14).[11] Many Bible scholars agree that the number twelve symbolizes the eschatological restoration of the twelve tribes of Israel.[12]

In summary, the apostles were a distinct group of Jesus's followers selected and appointed by the sovereign choice of Jesus after he had sought and received divine approval from his Father through prayer. Jesus called the twelve apostles for the ministry of apostleship, and they all responded in obedience to the call, realizing the purpose and the commitment it demanded. Jesus foresaw the future restoration of the twelve tribes of Israel through the twelve apostles.

The twelve apostles were called and appointed for a specific purpose – the ministry of apostleship. Craig Evans defines the word "apostle" as "one who is sent, usually as a messenger, agent, deputy, or ambassador. It was understood that an apostle was commissioned by a higher authority and acted in behalf of this authority."[13] The task for which Jesus chose the twelve disciples was communicated to them clearly right from the beginning.

Jesus's Purpose in the Calling and Appointment of the Twelve Apostles (Mark 3:14–15)

This second section seeks to determine why Jesus appointed the twelve apostles. Jesus's calling and appointment of the twelve apostles was purposeful. Therefore, both his training plan and his process were purpose oriented. Krallmann describes Jesus's purpose:

> The Master, furthermore, mentored for a mission. He, whom the Father has sent as a missionary into the world, instilled in

---

9. Guelich, *Mark 1–8*, 157.
10. Evans, "Mark," in *Eerdmans Commentary on the Bible* edited by Dunn and Rogerson, 1074.
11. Edwards, *Mark*, 115; Witherington, *Gospel of Mark*, 151.
12. France, *Gospel of Mark*, 158; Guelich, *Mark 1–8*, 158.
13. Evans, "Mark," 1074.

his associates a global vision, entrusted them with a commission to be his representatives to all the world and promised the Holy Spirit's enabling for the accomplishment of this task.[14]

Jesus selection of the twelve disciples was purposeful. The first purpose of the call was for an intimate relationship with him, and the second was empowerment for ministry.

The second purpose for which Jesus called and appointed the twelve apostles was to give them a new spiritual ministry. According to Mark, their ministry was twofold, namely to preach, and to possess the authority to drive out demons from people.[15] Jerry Camery-Hoggatt comments:

> The grammar of the passage suggests that the single commission carries two balanced charges: To preach and to drive out demons. The fact that driving out demons is an integral part of the apostolic commission may give the modern reader a pause, but we have already seen that Jesus' entire healing ministry should be understood as an act of vanquishing Satan. It would appear that for Mark's authorial reader, one could hardly hope to carry forward Jesus' program of the kingdom without in some way vanquishing Satan in Jesus' name.[16]

Jesus drove evil spirits out of people with authority (Mark 1:27). Jesus's ministry of driving out demons has a double effect. First, it delivers people who are possessed and oppressed by demonic forces. As such, this ministry involves liberation and relief from satanic bondage (Luke 13:16). Second, this ministry is a sign of victory over Satan and his kingdom (Matt 12:25–28).

The Identity of the Twelve Apostles as Individuals (Mark 3:16–19)

The third major unit of Mark 3:13–19 involves a listing of the twelve apostles. As a group, Jesus selected the twelve apostles from among the rest of his followers for the purpose of closer fellowship with him so he might give them a new spiritual identity (discipleship).[17] This new identity would prepare them

---

14. Krallmann, *Mentoring for Mission*, 15.
15. Witherington, *Gospel of Mark*, 151.
16. Camery-Hoggatt, "Mark" in *Life in the Spirit*, 290.
17. Edwards, *Mark*, 113.

for the new ministry (apostleship) so that they would be able to proclaim the good news of the kingdom of God and also dismantle the kingdom of Satan by delivering people from under his oppression. The twelve apostles can be categorized into five groups based on their respective individual identities and contributions to the group.[18] The first group consists of the most prominent apostles, namely Peter, James, and John. They were closely associated with Jesus in his ministry (Mark 5:37; 9:2; 14:33).[19] The second group consists of those apostles about whom Scripture offers little information regarding their respective identities and roles, namely Andrew, Philip, and Thomas. The third group consists of those whose respective identities and roles are debatable, namely Bartholomew, Matthew, and James the son of Alphaeus.[20] Bartholomew is identified with Nathanael by some Bible commentators although no reliable evidence exists (John 1:45).[21] Matthew is probably Levi, as many commentators assume. However, nothing is known about him except his call and his name in the list of the twelve apostles. James son of Alphaeus is associated with James "the younger" (Mark 15:40).[22] The fourth group consists of those about whom nothing is known except the inclusion of their names in lists of the twelve apostles, namely Simon the Zealot and Thadaeus (Judas son of James). Last comes Judas Iscariot, who betrayed Jesus and ended his life tragically.

There is a scarcity of biblical and extrabiblical evidence regarding the individual identities and roles of each of the twelve apostles. However, their collective group identity is more important than their respective individual identities. The collective name "the Twelve" is so significant in Scripture that even after the death of Judas Iscariot and before the replacement by Matthias, the group was known by this name (1 Cor 15:4). R. T. France concludes: "Several of the Twelve are quite unknown in the NT except as names on the list. Their corporate identity was more important than their individual profile."[23] The New Testament focuses more on the office and contribution of the twelve as apostles than on their roles as individuals.

---

18. France, *Gospel of Mark*, 162.
19. Keener, *New Testament*, 143.
20. Keck, *New Interpreter's Bible*, 18.
21. Guelich, *Mark 1–8*, 160.
22. Taylor, *St. Mark*, 234.
23. France, *Gospel of Mark*, 159.

The Training Experience of the Church in the Past

Leadership training has long been part of the church's ministry. Churches throughout Africa, Asia, Latin America, and the rest of the world have had both successes and limitations in the types of training programs they have designed to equip their leaders.

Examples from the History of the Global Church

Protestant evangelical churches in Ethiopia have inherited diverse kinds of church leadership styles introduced by Western missionaries. When missionaries pioneered most of the Protestant churches here in Ethiopia, they also transferred some of their leadership styles they practiced back home. Missionary Johnny Bakke has written about the impact of the missionary model of leadership on the history of the evangelical church in Ethiopia. According to Bakke, outlining the missionary model of leadership is difficult because the missionaries came from different backgrounds. In addition, the missionaries came from societies in which hierarchical models of leadership prevailed. Due to this hierarchical model of leadership, decision-making was centralized. Missionaries did not have uniform attitudes toward local culture. In spite of being targets of criticism, missionaries exemplified a leadership style in schools, clinics, hospitals, and evangelistic work.[24]

The historical development of the church in the West also impacted the development of church leadership in Ethiopia by importing secular values such as management models and political values such as the democratic process into church administration systems through training in higher theological institutions.[25] The adoption of secular and political models has resulted in the lack of a biblical and contextualized church leadership tradition or traditions. The evangelical churches in Ethiopia are experiencing spiritual and administrative turmoil because of inappropriate and inadequate leadership selection and development models, direct and indirect results of the historical development of leadership in the global church.[26] In light of Ethiopian and universal church history regarding the development of church leadership,

---

24. Bakke, "Models of Leadership," 156–57.
25. Elliston, *Home Grown Leaders*, 11.
26. Elliston, 46.

the need for alternative leadership training models that are culturally contextualized is significant.

The church in Africa has evolved through change, good and bad, during the years of its establishment in North Africa as well as during the years of expansion in the centuries that followed. At present, the evangelical church in Africa is growing numerically and geographically, although its spiritual growth rate does not match its need. The key problem for nongrowth in Africa is the issue of leadership. Tokunboh Adeyemo writes about the need for Christlike leadership in Africa: "Christlike leadership is needed in both the church and society in Africa. Such leadership will require purity of heart (God looks at the heart, not the head), passion for people, power to serve through prayer, a pioneering spirit, practical wisdom to solve problems and perseverance."[27]

Leadership development for the growing church in Africa has been a critical need in the past and is still a critical need today.

Lessons from the History of the Church in Ethiopia

The history of the universal church and of the church in Africa and in Ethiopia in particular reminds today's church leaders in this part of the world of an important fact regarding the training and development of church leaders. Leadership training is closely tied to the church's ability to be self-governing and self-supporting. Alternative leadership training that is culturally contextualized can be established only under an administratively self-governing and financially self-supporting church.

The history of the Protestant church in Ethiopia indicates the relationship between leadership training and the ability to be self-supporting. Bakke summarizes the effect of the missionary education program in Ethiopia:

> It is impossible to assess the full impact of education offered by the missions in the field of national leadership development.... Through their many schools the missions had a much greater impact on future Ethiopian leaders and models of leadership than the number of missionaries might imply. It is without doubt

---

27. Adeyemo, "Leadership," in *Africa Bible Commentary*, 546.

that it was in the field of education that missionaries had the most profound impact on leadership roles in Ethiopia.[28]

Christian missionaries from Europe and North America introduced a holistic ministry to Ethiopia in which the people of this nation benefited from the education, health, and development programs that were sponsored and implemented by these missionaries.

Western missionaries are the pioneers of modern education in Ethiopia. The people of Ethiopia are greatly indebted to them. The Catholic, Adventist, Protestant, and other Western missionary organizations have built schools and educated most of the present-day leaders both in the church and in society.[29] However, the impact of this missionary education was limited in producing effective and qualified church leaders. Bakke admits this limitation: "Schools which were started with the aim of prompting evangelism and church leadership often had a high number of students with no intention of joining the ministry."[30] One of the challenges for theological schools in Ethiopia to this day is that some of their graduates aspire either for higher education or jobs that can help them earn money. This tendency among theological school graduates has discouraged sponsoring churches and has also disappointed leaders of theological institutions.

Theological Doctrines Relevant to Alternative Leadership Training Models That Are Culturally Contextualized

The development of alternative leadership training models that are culturally contextualized initially requires the development of contextualized biblical theology to guide the overall ministry philosophy of a church.[31] The relevant theological tenets for these models include the doctrine of the Trinity, the doctrine of Christ, the doctrine of the Holy Spirit, the doctrine of humanity, the doctrine of the church, the doctrine of marriage, the doctrine of Satan, and the theology of ministry.

---

28. Bakke, "Models of Leadership," 164.
29. Bakke, "Models of Leadership," 164.
30. Bakke, 164.
31. Hiebert, *Anthropological Reflections*, 228.

A biblically balanced alternative leadership training model that is culturally contextualized in Ethiopia will include, first, the doctrine of the Trinity.[32] Ethiopia is a nation with multiethnic and multireligious groups. One of the challenges in such an environment involves maintaining the balance between unity and diversity. The doctrine of the Trinity comes into effect in such circumstances in order to shape the relationship among leaders and congregants.[33]

Second, the doctrine of Christ needs to be revisited in the context of Ethiopian evangelical churches. In general, the understanding of the church in Ethiopia is that Jesus performed his signs and miracles as a result of being anointed by the Holy Spirit. The Western theology of the non-charismatic Christ, according to some authors, is not relevant in Ethiopia. John F. Walvoord writes about the divine attributes of the Son of God, especially his omnipotence:

> The evidence for the omnipotence of Christ is as decisive as proof for other attributes. Sometimes it takes the form of physical power, but more often it refers to authority over creation. Christ has the power . . . to heal physically, as witnessed by His many miracles, as well as power to cast out demons (Mark 1:29–34).[34]

But some Christians assert that Jesus's healings and miracles were not demonstrations of his deity but instead a result of his anointing by the Holy Spirit (Luke 4:17–19; Acts 10:38). Roger Stronstad associates Jesus's and the disciples' miracle-working power with the anointing of the Holy Spirit:

> The power of the Spirit is miracle-working power, not only in the ministry of Jesus, but also for the disciples. Thus, having received the power of the Spirit on the day of Pentecost, the disciples heal the sick (Acts 3:1ff.; 9:32ff.), raise the dead (Acts 9:36ff.), and do many other signs and wonders (Acts 2:43; 4:33 et al.). Indeed as God had earlier anointed Jesus with the Holy Spirit and power, with the result that he went about doing good and

---

32. Hiebert, 228–31.
33. Meyers, "Trinitarian Vision," 67.
34. Walvoord, *Jesus Christ Our Lord*, 29.

healing all who were oppressed by the devil, so God baptized the disciples with the Holy Spirit and power, so that they also went about doing good and healing all who were oppressed by the devil, for the Spirit of God was with them.[35]

Therefore, the doctrine of the charismatic Christ, whose anointing by the Spirit is paradigmatic of the experience and ministry of the twelve apostles and the subsequent generation, is relevant to leadership training programs in Ethiopia. Christ is God who became human as the anointed messenger of his Father. His mission on earth is realized when Christian leaders understand that he was human, anointed by God with the Holy Spirit to empower him to accomplish this mission.

Third, the doctrine of the work of the Holy Spirit is also relevant in the leadership training programs among the evangelical churches of Ethiopia.[36] The churches in Ethiopia have experienced and enjoyed the charismatic work of the Holy Spirit uninterrupted for decades. The charismatic visitation of the Holy Spirit has penetrated all denominational boundaries, empowering both the ecumenical and the evangelical churches.[37] The evangelical churches in Ethiopia believe that this work of the Holy Spirit is scriptural and contemporary. Stronstad summarizes the timeless truth about the charismatic work of the Holy Spirit:

> To sum up, Luke's Pneumatology serves and complements his Christology. We have demonstrated that Jesus' experience of the Holy Spirit from his Jordan experience onwards is a paradigm for the disciples' experience of the Holy Spirit from Pentecost onwards. . . . There are clear implications from Luke's charismatic theology for the contemporary church. If the gift of the Spirit was charismatic or vocational for Jesus and the early church, so it ought to have a vocational dimension in the experience of God's people today.[38]

---

35. Stronstad, *Spirit, Scripture and Theology*, 162–63.
36. Elliston, *Home Grown Leaders*, 99.
37. Hege, *Beyond Our Prayers*, 244.
38. Stronstad, *Spirit, Scripture and Theology*, 166–67.

A sound and relevant theology of the person and work of the Holy Spirit needs to be developed for the evangelical churches in Ethiopia in order to direct the charismatic work of the Holy Spirit in a manner that will edify the church and glorify God.

The work of the Holy Spirit is needed right from the very beginning in the selection process of leaders and trainees. Jesus's example of seeking divine guidance during the calling and appointment of the twelve apostles sets the standard for selecting workers for the harvest. Edgar J. Elliston summarizes the overall role of the Holy Spirit in leadership development: "The Holy Spirit's initializing and integrating role is a crucial part of every stage of the leadership development process – selection, equipping, maturing, transitions, working through a person to equip others, bringing first a sense of destiny and then a sense of fulfillment as one's giftedness and role converge."[39]

A scriptural understanding of the nature and operation of the spiritual gifts is required for a healthy leadership training program. At the same time, believers need to avoid the two extremes of quenching the fire (1 Thess 5:19) and introducing "unauthorized fire" (Lev 10:1). Church leadership in the New Testament represents a call and empowerment from God through the Holy Spirit. Each church leader is considered as one among equals.

Fourth, relevant teaching regarding the doctrine of humanity needs an interpretive framework for leadership training.[40] Three major issues need to be resolved from a biblical perspective in order to shape the leaders of churches in Ethiopia. These issues are the holistic nature and needs of the human being, gender roles in church leadership, and ethnicity.

The human being is created in the image of the triune God, being one and many in composition. The individual is a unified being composed of both material and immaterial elements. A theology that overemphasizes one element over the other is not sound. Ethiopia is struggling to minimize poverty and poverty-related problems. Over 80 percent of the population live in rural areas with subsistence farming as their source of income. Alternative leadership training models that are culturally contextualized must address not only the holistic nature of humankind but the holistic needs of the human being as well.

---

39. Elliston, *Home Grown Leaders*, 99.
40. Grudem, *Systematic Theology*, 473.

Another significant theological issue related to the doctrine of humanity is the role of men and women in church ministry and leadership.[41] At creation, man and woman came equally from the hand of God the creator. In redemption, Christ loved the entire human race and died for all people. Therefore, in Christ, neither male nor female has relevance in regard to status. God also promised to pour out his Spirit upon men and women equally for the purpose of ministry (Gen 1:26; Gal 3:28; Acts 2:17–21). However, many cultures in Ethiopia unfortunately still have a low view of women, and this has affected the overall involvement of women in ministry, especially the ministry of church leadership. An alternative leadership training that is culturally contextualized should have the purpose of elevating the spiritual status of redeemed women to a biblical standard so that ministry becomes gift based as found in the New Testament, rather than gender oriented.

The third factor under the doctrine of humankind is ethnicity. As stated previously, Ethiopia is a land of diverse people groups and cultures. Tribalism is a critical issue in the selection of leaders. A continuous reminder of the biblical understanding of ethnicity is needed for healthy relationships.[42] At one extreme, ethnocentrism undermines people of other ethnic identities, and at the other extreme, hypernationalism denies ethnic identity.[43]

Fifth, the doctrine of the church needs to be revised in the context of the Ethiopian cultural and social setting.[44] One of the strengths of the evangelical churches in Ethiopia concerns active evangelism and the subsequent church planting. A critical issue for leadership training in the area of the doctrine of the church is the corporate nature of the call. The corporate call of the apostles was more significant than the individual identity of each apostle. In the same manner, God called his people, in both the Old and the New Testaments, corporately (Exod 19:5–6; 1 Pet 2:9–10).

The relationship between leaders and congregants connects with the corporate nature of the Christian community. Some of the secular values of the management model of leadership have penetrated churches' administration

---

41. Grudem, *Systematic Theology*, 456.
42. Gangel, *Team Leadership*, 30.
43. Pohor, "Tribalism Ethnicity and Race," 316.
44. Fee, *Gospel and Spirit*, 129.

systems here in Ethiopia, and as a result, a hierarchy is evident between leaders and followers as well as among leaders with different roles.[45]

The church in Ethiopia needs Christian leaders who have biblical, historical, and contemporary knowledge of the nature and function of the church both as the universal body of Christ and as a local congregation, which is the true expression of that body here on earth.[46]

Sixth, the doctrine of marriage is a significant topic in light of the multiethnic cultural values and traditional practices that exist in Ethiopia. Polygyny, widow inheritance, and divorce and remarriage all have a significant negative impact on church leadership in many cultures and societies in Ethiopia. These practices are prevalent in the church also. Mae Alice Regggy-Mamo explains the practice of widow inheritance in Africa Bible Commentary as follows:

> In the African tradition, several types of marital unions are open to a widow. In one of them, a widow becomes the legal wife of a close relative of the dead husband. The children of this union inherit through the new husband, who is their legal father. This custom is called widow inheritance.[47]

These practices greatly affect the selection and appointment of leaders. Churches in Ethiopia need to maintain the biblical standard for the spiritual and moral qualifications of leaders in spite of all cultural pressures (Mal 2:16; Matt 19:9; 1 Tim 3:2). According to the writer of Hebrews, "marriage should be honored by all, and the marriage bed kept pure, for God will judge the adulterer and all the sexually immoral" (13:4). One task awaiting evangelical leaders in Ethiopia is to conduct research into the cultural values of marriage that are held by the diverse ethnic groups in the country.

Seventh, biblical demonology requires revisiting by theologians.[48] One of God's commandments to the children of Israel was to abstain from any demonic practices which were prevalent in Egypt and Canaan at that time. God warned the children of Israel against all practice of witchcraft: "Let no one be found among you who sacrifices their son or daughter in the fire, who practices divination or sorcery, interprets omens, engages in witchcraft, or

---

45. Hodges, *Church Planting*, 79–83.
46. Horton, *Systematic Theology*, 539.
47. Reggy-Mamo, "Widow Inheritance" in *Africa Bible Commentary*, 323.
48. Hiebert, *Anthropological Reflections*, 238.

casts spells, or who is a medium or spiritist or who consults the dead" (Deut 18:10–11). Although this warning was given nearly four thousand years ago, such practices are still prevalent in Ethiopia and throughout Africa.[49]

Thus, biblical demonology in the Ethiopian/African context should be part of the course contents of alternative leadership training that is culturally contextualized. Christian leaders in the evangelical churches of Ethiopia need to be instructed in sound theology regarding the nature and work of demons in order to avoid the extremes of either fear of demons or denial of the operation of evil forces in the world. However, believers are also encouraged to exercise freedom from excessive fear of demons. Believers are empowered to help and pray for those who are suffering under the bondage of Satan.[50]

Eighth, a theology of ministry needs to be developed to create a biblical awareness of the holistic nature of God's mission. Confusion exists between the spiritual and the secular, ministry and work, among evangelical leaders in Ethiopia. The word for "secular" in Amharic is *alemawi*, which means "worldly." A New Testament understanding of the theology of ministry is essential.

As mentioned previously, 82 percent of the Ethiopian population lives and works in rural areas. Most of the evangelical churches are located in these rural villages and towns. Every citizen in the rural areas is a member of the peasant association. Pastors, evangelists, teachers, and other leaders of rural churches are members of these associations. The words "full-time," "part-time," "clergy," and "laity" are relative terms in such contexts. The pastors, evangelists, teachers, and other leaders are "full-time" workers while still living on their farms and fulfilling their agricultural obligations to society and the state. Alternative leadership training models that are culturally contextualized will consider these elements when designing the curriculum.[51] A popular saying in Ethiopia is, "You can plough an indigenous soil effectively only by using indigenous oxen." Developing alternative leadership training that is culturally contextualized represents both a need and a challenge. The need is expressed in multidimensional ways by the leadership, the congregants, and even the community. Transforming the traditional ways of training as well as improving the leadership models requires time and tolerance. In spite

---

49. Kunhiyop, "Witchcraft," 374.
50. Kunhiyop, 374.
51. Degefa, *Yehiwot Wuquir*, 271.

of all these challenges and hindrances, I believe that introducing alternative training models to discontinue ineffective methods and to redeem emerging leaders for God's mission in the nation is a timely pursuit. I see my role as similar to that of Nehemiah, who played a vital leadership role in nation building. The evangelical churches in Ethiopia currently need leaders willing to pay the full price to serve as a buffer between the old and the new generation of Christian leaders. My role in the implementation of alternative leadership training that is culturally contextualized is that of program developer. According to Robert E. Ferris, the task of the program developer involves the following elements:

1. The developer shall have a vision for training in his or her own context;
2. The training developer conceives and implements training strategies;
3. The developer possesses authority to initiate toward launching or modifying leadership training;
4. The program developer will be engaged in coordinating program development activities; and
5. The developer provides a unifying vision and leadership for the overall task.[52]

The foundational principles discussed from Scripture, systematic theology, and church history in this work provide a guide and an interpretive framework for the development of alternative leadership training that is culturally contextualized for evangelical churches in Ethiopia.

This literature review next discusses two major topics: first, past and present models of leadership training in Ethiopia; and, second, African and global trends in church leadership training. Some key terms and concepts require definition and description in assessing the need for these training models for evangelical churches in Ethiopia with a focus on the Hiwot Berhan Church of Ethiopia.

---

52. Ferris, *Ministry Training*, 3.

Alternative Leadership Training That Is Culturally Contextualized

The primary source in assessing the need for church leadership training models is the Christian community – the existing leadership and congregants living and serving in a specific geographical location.[53] In this ministry project, the broader cultural context is the nation of Ethiopia with its over eighty major ethnic groups and languages. The narrower cultural context is the Hiwot Berhan Church of Ethiopia, which has worked among diversified ethnic groups for the last fifty-four years.[54] Alternative leadership training that is culturally contextualized takes into consideration the worldview, social values, language, economic status, tradition, art, music, and communication methods of the community required to transmit information and tradition.[55]

Church Leadership Training Model(s)

This ministry project utilizes the phrase "church leadership training model" in two ways. First, the phrase refers to the existing theological institutions operating in Ethiopia to prepare Christian workers for the church and the community. These theological institutions are mostly formal academic institutions with curricula designed either by missionaries from Western countries or by nationals according to the Western model of curriculum development. Second, the phrase is used for the proposed training models with an indigenous input regarding the content and means of delivery for church leadership training specifically for the Hiwot Berhan Church of Ethiopia and also for the evangelical churches in Ethiopia. The research outcome could indicate the need to embrace either partially or fully the Western formal model of church leadership training as it exists now in Ethiopia; alternatively, the research outcome might fully reject the Western model of formal education to train church leaders in Ethiopia. However, the important issue in this project is to explore the expressed needs of church leaders and congregants representing their churches, the rest of church leaders, and their respective communities.[56]

---

53. Tennent, *World Missions*, 347–53.
54. Hiebert, *Anthropological Reflections*, 88–89, 101–2.
55. Fuliga, "Problems in Theological Education," 287.
56. Hatiya, "Yeethiopia Hiwot Berhan," 22, 26.

The Hiwot Berhan Church of Ethiopia

The evangelical churches in Ethiopia came together in 1976 during the Communist regime in order to establish an underground national fellowship to maintain spiritual unity to reach previously unreached people with the gospel and to seek legal recognition from the government.[57] Currently, the Evangelical Churches Fellowship of Ethiopia (ECFE) is a registered and state-recognized national fellowship that publicly represents the needs of evangelicals. The Hiwot Berhan Church of Ethiopia was one of the nine founding members of the Evangelical Churches Fellowship of Ethiopia when the fellowship was established in 1976. I believe that the training needs explored in one of the member churches of the fellowship will also reflect the needs of other member churches because they are all serving the same community – people groups and languages in Ethiopia.

History of Theological Education in Ethiopia

Although Ethiopia has never been colonized by Western powers, both its secular and its religious educational systems have been designed after the Western model of education. Western missionaries designed the theological education systems. The theological trainings by Western missionaries misinformed the native learners about tradition, social and cultural values, the communal way of life, decision-making processes by consensus, the existing religious values of the Ethiopian Orthodox Tewahedo Church, and the preservation of cultural and natural heritage. Western theology in its early phase in Ethiopia considered almost everything in the tradition as heathen and demonic. As such, Western theology destroyed some of the traditional leadership structure, attempting to substitute it with the Western democratic style of leadership. As a result of the missionary's teaching, native evangelists instructed new converts to abandon ancestral grave sites, to remove objects of worship such as trees, drums, etc., and to stop grieving for the dead. In its four-hundred-year history, the Western type of theological education neither touched nor was able to remove many harmful cultural and social practices in Ethiopia, such as female genital mutilation and polygamous marriage. The Ethiopian Orthodox Tewahedo Church set an example in establishing the

---

57. Hege, *Beyond Our Prayers*, 166.

oldest theological institution in Ethiopia. Its schools train clergy for ministry within the church and the community. These theological schools follow the master-disciple model in which learners come to a learning center run by a scholar.[58] Instruction occurs in the vernacular, and the scholar imparts knowledge orally as well as through the sacred Scriptures.[59] The students learn by rote. They are required to imitate their mentor in character and skill. The courses in these schools for the priesthood include literacy, the Scriptures, liturgy, poetry, and music.[60]

Western missionaries did make valuable contributions in Ethiopia by introducing modern education that prepared and produced nationals who rose even to become heads of state.[61] Catholics, Protestants, and Adventists have established and run numerous elementary, secondary, and postsecondary schools (i.e. colleges) both in rural Ethiopia and in urban areas;[62] these promoted the livelihoods of citizens and also prepared many for effective civil service.[63]

Western mission schools used a holistic approach to teach students both the sciences and the Scriptures. Conduct was emphasized as a qualification for promotion or for reward for academic excellence. Many of the graduates from these mission schools have become heads of state, parliamentarians, lawmakers, ministers, and politicians. However, these schools were limited in that their graduates lacked direct involvement in church ministry, as the missionaries had intended.[64]

Degree granting seminaries, colleges and training centers in Ethiopia that have departments and majors for leadership are designed after Western models and their medium of instructions is foreign to the learners.[65]

Another contemporary trend in leadership training in Ethiopia concerns churches and Christian organizations with a mixed model of training in which both the curriculum and the medium of instruction use one of the

---

58. Kassaye, "Curriculum Development," 52–53.
59. Ullendorff, *Ethiopians*, 200–3.
60. Wondimagegnehu and Motovu, *Ethiopian Orthodox Church*, 127–28.
61. Haile, Lande, and Rubenson, *Missionary Factor*, 155–56.
62. G/Ammanuel, *Church and Missions*, 332–39.
63. Alberto, *Apostolic Vicariate of Galla*, 258–60.
64. Haile, Lande, and Rubenson, *Missionary Factor*, 164.
65. Biza, "Servant-Leadership Development," 108–12.

vernaculars – Amharic. Some churches and theological institutions run their diploma- and certificate-level theological education in Amharic in order to make the program accessible to more people. These institutions conduct theological education by extension (TEE) in the Amharic language. For the purposes of this project, I describe these programs as espousing a mixed model because although the medium of instruction used by these institutions is the vernacular, the curriculum of each institution is still adopted from the Western models of theological education designed in English. They all struggle regarding the relevancy of content and the contextualization of methodology.

Training programs conducted for church leadership in Ethiopia are highly recommended to take into consideration the actual context of the community. According to the report by the Central Statistical Agency of Ethiopia, in 2007 the literacy rate in Ethiopia was 39.8 percent. The country is large and mountainous, and some places are still inaccessible by road. Infrastructure and technological advancements are still in progress. The people's livelihood is in farming and cattle breeding. The diversity of ethnicity and language is an essential factor to consider when designing and conducting theological training. The status of women at home, in the church, and in the community needs to be elevated through education and advocacy. Most of the Christian workers in Ethiopian evangelical churches are bivocational, and leadership trainings must also take this into consideration.[66]

Theological Education/Leadership Training Model(s) in Ethiopia Compared with Model(s) in Other Regions of the World

The need for alternative and culturally contextualized leadership training programs is a critical issue common to churches and theological institutions working in Majority World countries. Churches and theological institutions in Africa, Asia, and Latin America are undertaking all kinds of surveys and research to make theological training in their respective regions relevant, sustainable, and accessible.

---

66. Biza, 108–12.

Africa

The history of early African Christianity demonstrates that African church leaders and scholars trained other Africans for the ministry. The establishment of the School of Alexandria in Egypt and of the School of Carthage in North Africa provide examples of self-supporting and self-governing theological training in the church in Africa in its early stages.[67] However, history also describes how colonialism later introduced a type of culturally irrelevant theological education as well as modern education.[68] Ogbu U. Kalu summarizes the limitations of the Western models of theological education in African settings:

> The curricula undermined indigenous values and cultural traditions. . . . It rejected local traditional power and authority structures, and set out to create new leadership and ministerial systems along European lines. The preference for residential or walled institutions had many advantages that enhanced – but removed the students from their world and its wealth of indigenous knowledge.[69]

This trend of dislocating trainees from their cultural roots is one of the obstacles theological institutions and churches in Ethiopia are still struggling to overcome in order to attract as many trainees as possible to their leadership training programs.

Theological training during the colonial period in Africa primarily served the interests of the trainers rather than the needs of the trainees.[70] In addition, both the curriculum and the medium of instruction were foreign to the native African learner.[71] The theological training was aimed at creating native puppets who faithfully but blindly imitated their foreign missionary trainers.[72] Since the models of theological training were so formal that they were given in a classroom setting, they were not accessible to the majority of Christian workers, nor did they take into consideration the cultural and social setting of

---

67. Shaw, *African Christianity*, 32.
68. Hiebert, *Anthropological Reflections*, 76–78.
69. Kalu, "Elijah's Mantle," 269.
70. Kalu, 269.
71. Gatwa, "Theological Education," 202.
72. Anderson, "Fury and Wonder," 288.

the African community.[73] Theological education in the colonial era abolished many harmless traditions, customs, methods of communication, means of entertainment, and elements of heritage.[74] Finally, the colonial system encouraged total dependency on foreign programs, support, and methodologies, and it did not encourage the use of indigenous resources.[75]

Some of the current leadership training programs in Africa are offered by theological colleges owned and operated by Western mission organizations, ecumenical theological institutions, denominational theological colleges, Christian universities, leadership training centers, and TEE programs.

Accordingly, the church in Africa has struggled to make church leadership training relevant and effective. One area of struggle has been finding an acceptable holistic approach that will address the spiritual, social, political, and economic needs of the society. A second area needing improvement is contextualizing the curricula through the use of indigenous languages, staff, and teaching materials.[76] Third, being self-supporting by using domestic resources so that institutions do not develop a dependency on foreign resources has been the greatest challenge of all.[77] Fourth, elevating the status of women at home, in the church, and in the community so that they can play significant leadership roles is another area in which the church needs development.[78]

The church in Africa needs to consider several societal conditions in order to become effective in developing alternative leadership training models that are culturally contextualized for church leaders. These conditions include the rate of literacy among the rural society, the low opinion of women, the high level of poverty, the role of elders in the community, and the wasted potential of the youth both in the church and in society.

Several trends in churches and theological institutions in Africa demonstrate efforts to resolve the challenges related to indigenization and meet the regional and global demands to fulfill God's mission.[79] African theologians, scholars, writers, and international leaders are beginning to produce literature

---

73. Kalu, "Elijah's Mantle," 270.
74. Draper and Ruddoch, "Ministerial Formation," 11.
75. Gatwa, "Theological Education," 193.
76. Kalu, "Elijah's Mantle," 270.
77. Draper and Ruddoch, "Ministerial Formation," 10.
78. Girma, "Women in Leadership," 71.
79. Gatwa, "Theological Education," 205.

that addresses the contemporary spiritual, social, political, and economic issues on the continent.[80] Furthermore, churches and theological institutions in Africa are beginning to evaluate the content, context, and methodology of Western theological education and make several adjustments.[81] Specifically, Western theological education does not follow a holistic approach;[82] it is not needs based, but is developed to resolve problems in the Western context;[83] it has a medium of instruction foreign to most African target groups;[84] it encourages denominationalism rather than ecumenicalism;[85] it creates a divide between the clergy and the laity;[86] and it leads to an economic dependency on foreign support.[87] In addition, African churches and theological institutions are elevating the role of women in church leadership[88] and writing Christian literature for Africans by Africans, as evidenced by the *Africa Bible Commentary*, written by seventy African authors.[89] Furthermore, African churches and theological institutions are developing alternative church leadership training models that are contextual, holistic, relational, experiential, and cost effective.[90] In addition, Ethiopian churches and theological institutions are partnering with churches and Christian institutions in the West with mutual understanding and benefit. African church leaders are both training and being trained in the West, and Western leaders are being trained and are training in African institutions. By establishing Christian universities with the purpose of developing a holistic approach, many African churches including those in Ethiopia are addressing the spiritual, social, political, and economic aspects of the society.[91] Furthermore, Ethiopian churches and theological institutions are upholding the traditional community leadership values by reaching the elders of the community to empower them for church

---

80. Simiyu, "Christian Leadership Development," 65.
81. Anderson, "Fury and Wonder," 288.
82. Banwell, "Christian Witness."
83. Elliston, "Masai Leadership Development," 29.
84. Gatwa, "Theological Education," 193.
85. Girma, "Women in Leadership," 21.
86. Kalu, "Elijah's Mantle," 269.
87. Nürnberger, "Ministerial Training," 76.
88. Girma, "Women in Leadership," 21.
89. Adeyemo, *Africa Bible Commentary*.
90. Mejia, "Training for Religious."
91. Kalu, "Elijah's Mantle," 275.

leadership,[92] and by viewing the church as a charismatic community of the Holy Spirit and the body of Christ in which the divide between the clergy and the laity is dismantled.[93]

Asia

The church in Asia has much to offer to the church in Ethiopia and to the wider context of the church in Africa in training substance, method, and resources, as evidenced by the Korean church ministry of sending missionaries to theological institutions and Christian universities in Africa. The Korean Presbyterian Church is providing a holistic ministry to the people of Ethiopia through its Christian hospital located in Addis Ababa. Both operating in the Majority World, the churches in Africa and Asia share common challenges. These challenges include the Westernization of theological education models, religious pluralism, financial dependency on the West, the struggle for the indigenization of methodology and the contextualization of the contents of theological education, and "the brain-drain from the South to the North" of native theologians.[94]

Churches in Asia and Africa are working independently of each other and yet are benefiting by learning from each other in three main areas. First, they are both evaluating the limitations of Western models of theological training and as a result are realizing the need for change in both the content and the method of training church leaders. Jose B. Fuliga concludes his evaluation of the existing Western models of training in Asia saying, "The Third World theological institutions in following the Western church and its theology have failed to harness the wealth of their indigenous theological expression and imagination as evident in their music and ways of worship."[95] Second, churches on both continents are designing and implementing culturally oriented, relevant, and cost-effective alternative training models for their churches, accessible to both vocational and bivocational leaders.[96] Finally, churches in Asia and Africa are applying the charismatic approach in training

---

92. Kalu, 269.
93. Fee, *Gospel and Spirit*, 120–43.
94. Fuliga, "Problems in Theological Education," 287.
95. Fuliga, 287.
96. Kalu, "Elijah's Mantle," 270.

church leaders. The charismatic approach realizes the church is a community of the Holy Spirit. Leaders are oriented to worship and ministry inspired by the charismatic work of the Holy Spirit. To that end, preaching the Word in power accompanied by signs and wonders is encouraged. In addition, the charismatic approach to leadership training dismantles the cultural value that leadership gives status; instead, this approach abolishes the divide between clergy and laity, introduces gift-based servant leadership, and unifies the church as the body of Christ.[97]

Latin America

The church in Latin America is currently making progress regarding developing alternative leadership training that is culturally contextualized. To that end, the Latin American church is evaluating the pros and cons of the Western models of theological education and analyzing both the content and the means of delivery. In addition, they are analyzing their own political, social, religious, and economic contexts with a focus on reaching the poor and the victims of political and social injustice, and are developing culturally oriented, holistic, and charismatic alternative training models for church leaders.[98] Aharon Sapsezian recommends the TEE style of training for church leaders in Latin America, and his justification applies even to churches in Ethiopia:

> Understandably, the TEE structure and method suit the ministerial need of these churches, as most of the trainees are mature, self-supporting persons with some sort of leadership responsibility in their respective congregations, and could not afford the time, the cost, and formalities of a protracted residential programme away from their localities.[99]

Distance education is one of the alternative leadership training models that has proven to be effective for its accessibility to most training candidates in Majority World countries. However, one of its limitations is that it does not reach the illiterate population with oral tradition.

---

97. Anderson, "Fury and Wonder," 293–96.
98. Sapsezian, "Ministry with the Poor," 6.
99. Sapsezian, 6.

Catholicism, Protestantism, and Pentecostalism dominate the church in Latin America. The political, social, and economic oppression Latin Americans experienced under Western colonial powers gave rise to the formation and response of liberation theology. Liberation theology represents the church's reaction to poverty and injustice caused by unjust government systems and by the advocates of capitalism within Latin American society.[100]

The Pentecostal charismatic movement had a direct impact on the suffering society in Latin America. Pentecostalism in Latin America dismantled the clergy-laity divide in the church and elevated the status of women at home, in church, and in society. Furthermore, the Pentecostal charismatic approach focused on reaching the poor and the marginalized in society and impacted the arenas of politics, the public, and the media.[101]

The content and method of theological education in Latin America are being designed to be indigenous, holistic, and community oriented.[102] The Latin American practice of a holistic approach through a Pentecostal orientation has a counterpart in Africa, also. Churches in Africa are experiencing the Pentecostal charismatic type of approach, enabling them to develop a holistic approach to ministry in order to meet the needs of the Christian community as well as the society.[103]

The evangelical churches in Ethiopia experienced religious restrictions and a series of severe persecutions during the imperial regime (1930–74) and the Communist regime (1974–91). The religious hardship brought different evangelical denominations together and unified them in worship, purpose, and ministry. As mentioned earlier, nine evangelical denominations established the Evangelical Churches Fellowship of Ethiopia in 1976.[104] These interdenominational and interchurch fellowships created a charismatic and ecumenical environment among local congregations through the sovereign work of the Holy Spirit. The charismatic approach to ministry in Ethiopia has minimized the clergy-laity divide and instead has encouraged a gifts-based ministry of all believers in which both vocational and bivocational leaders are

---

100. Sapsezian, 5.
101. Gooren, "Pentecostalization," 368.
102. Sapsezian, "Ministry with the Poor," 6.
103. Anderson, "Fury and Wonder," 293.
104. Hege, *Beyond Our Prayers*, 166, 244.

part of church governance. The context of the charismatic approach will be considered in exploring and developing alternative leadership training that is culturally contextualized for church leaders in the Hiwot Berhan Church as well as the rest of the evangelical churches in Ethiopia.

Churches in Africa, Asia, and Latin America are experiencing the presence and active participation of a large population of young people in their congregations, which represents at the same time a blessing, an opportunity, and a challenge for the churches in these continents. This blessing fulfills God's promise to pour out his Spirit upon children and young people (Joel 2:28–32; Acts 2:17–21) to empower them for ministry (Acts 1:8). The presence of young people in churches represents an opportunity to embrace and nurture them for leadership to become today's coworkers and tomorrow's successors of the church of Christ. However, this opportunity can be a challenge if existing church leaders do not harness the leadership potential of young people through training, nurturing, and involving them in ministry.

The West

Andrew F. Walls summarizes the mutual task of churches in the West and in the Majority World: "We have a cultural task: Christ is to penetrate the traditions of thought of Africa and Asia and Latin America; Christ is to break into Western secular society. We are called to disciple nations."[105] Churches and theological institutions in the Western hemisphere are making progress in the process of contextualizing their theological education models in light of their exposure to global culture and their determination to accommodate non-Western cultures and theologies. They are demonstrating a transformational attitude and constructive involvement in their approach to Majority World cultures.[106] In addition, churches and theological institutions in the West are embracing immigrants from Majority World countries and are encouraging multiculturalism. The church in diaspora composed of persons from the Majority World is making a significant impact in reaching Western society with the gospel cross-culturally. Furthermore, churches and theological institutions that are attempting to maintain the balance are revising

---

105. Walls, "World Christianity," 240.
106. Tennent, *World Missions*, 347–53.

their curricula, increasing the number of new admissions from non-Western countries, integrating non-Western staff, and accepting and respecting theologies designed in non-Western contexts. The churches are accommodating multilingual services in their churches.[107]

As the body of Christ, the church has a universal scope and mission. Furthermore, the church is not western, eastern, southern, or northern in its identity. The universal church is not geographically, ethnically, or racially divided. The terms west and east, south and north, African and European, stand for the cultural contexts in which the body of Christ is expressing itself as local congregations for the purpose of fulfilling its God-given mission on earth.

The body of Christ that is operating in the western, eastern, southern, and northern parts of the globe is still organically one entity. The church operating in all cultures has the same biblical mandate of training – equipping the saints with a mission. The churches in Europe and North America are privileged with theological tradition, training expertise, and material resources. The churches in Majority World nations are privileged with potential human resources, historical and cultural heritage, and untapped material resources. The mission of God to the world is accomplished neither by the church in the Minority World alone nor by the church in the Majority World alone. God's mission is accomplished only when the churches in the Majority World and the Minority World give their right hand of fellowship to each other and realize their unity in mission within the diversity of their cultures (Gal 2:1–10).

Summary

Jesus included several elements in his model of training the Twelve as described in the gospels, such as purpose, selection criteria, the central kingdom message, teaching methods, empowerment for ministry, and domestic resources for training. As the literature shows, the leadership training models in Ethiopia and the rest of Africa as well as in Asia and Latin America have mostly been traditional, formal, and foreign models duplicated and adopted from Western civilization through the missionaries who initially pioneered the work in these parts of the world. Although these Western theological

---

107. Walls, "World Christianity," 239–40.

education models have proven constructive at times in the past, they still contrast sharply with Jesus's model of training as demonstrated in Scripture. The vast volume of literature on the topic of leadership training proves that churches and scholars in Majority World countries struggle to develop alternative leadership training that is culturally contextualized for their respective Christian communities. Theologians in these countries agree that the leadership training models for church leaders must be Bible based, Jesus modeled, church owned, and community oriented. Alternative leadership training that is culturally contextualized must take into consideration such aspects as the biblical and Jesus's model of training workers, the needs of the church and the community, the relevancy of the contents of the training, the contextualization of the training methods, the giftedness of Christian leaders, the principle of being self-supporting in training resources, and the use of vernaculars as a medium of instruction. The Western model of training is in sharp contrast to Jesus's model of training because the purpose, content, methods, and resources of Western models did not originate from the indigenous church and community. Instead, Western models were duplicated, at times without any critical evaluation. In this ministry project, I hope to join researchers, scholars, theologians, and educators from Majority World churches as well as the global church in the spiritual and intellectual struggle to develop alternative culturally relevant and economically sustainable leadership training models for church leaders.

A single model of church leadership training is impractical. Culture changes, as does the context. Target groups change as generations of believers come and go. The needs of the community also are subject to change as time passes; therefore, leadership training models must meet the new demands and needs of the church and community. Accordingly, leaders need to focus on identifying a biblical framework for developing alternative leadership training that is culturally contextualized in every generation.

Table 2.1 summarizes the content of the literature review by comparing and contrasting the theological training models in Africa, Asia, Latin America, and the West.

Table 2.1 Summary of the Literature Review

Topics	Africa	Asia	Latin America	West
Curriculum	Mostly adopted from Western cultures	Mostly adopted from Western cultures	Mostly adopted from Western cultures	Designed by professionals/ dichotomous
Models of trainings	Mostly adopted from Western cultures	Mostly adopted from Western cultures	Mostly adopted from Western cultures	Formal and informal
Medium of instruction	Foreign to most learners	Foreign to most learners	Researcher's knowledge limited	Native language
Affiliation	Evangelical, charismatic, ecumenical	Evangelical, charismatic, ecumenical	Evangelical, charismatic, ecumenical	Researcher's knowledge limited
Finance	Mostly dependent on foreign donations	Mostly dependent on foreign support	Researcher's knowledge limited	Domestic support
Teaching methods	Teacher centered/lecture dominated	Teacher centered/lecture dominated	Teacher centered/lecture dominated	Diversified
Trainees	Mostly mature and in-service trainees	Researcher's knowledge limited	Researcher's knowledge limited	At the beginning of ministry
Training materials	Scarce in national languages; mostly in foreign language	Researcher's knowledge limited	Researcher's knowledge limited	Relevant and adequate
Awards	Duplication from Western cultures	Duplication from Western cultures	Duplication from Western cultures	Diplomas and degrees
Outcome	Well informed but poorly formed church elites	Researcher's knowledge limited	Researcher's knowledge limited	Researcher's knowledge limited

Research Design

My research was qualitative because it aimed at exploring a central phenomenon, namely alternative leadership training models that are culturally contextualized for evangelical church leaders in Ethiopia, with a specific focus on the Hiwot Berhan Church of Ethiopia. According to Tim Sensing, "qualitative research systematically seeks answers to questions by examining various social settings and the individuals who inhabit these settings."[108] I examined the training elements for church leadership in the context and setting of four cultural church groups.

Evaluative Research Method

I chose an evaluative research method for my research design. The qualitative evaluation method "is a type of social research that seeks to discover social reality, to probe its capacity for change and to test its boundaries, and on that seeks to change and create social reality."[109] In my ministry project the evaluative method is applied by presenting a comparison and contrast between the existing theological training models and the anticipated alternative training models that are culturally contextualized. The evaluation includes training components such as the relevancy of the contents of the curricula, the contextualization of delivery methods, the self-supporting nature of the program, and the outcome of the training. The data collection methods I used were focus group interviews, semistructured individual interviews, gathered documents, and observation. The focus groups were selected from four cultural groups. This research project focused on exploring the necessary elements that would support alternative leadership training programs for church leaders in Ethiopia.

A focus group is a research design that uses group interviews to gather data. According to Sensing, a focus group involves the following components. First, the researcher imposes the research theme.[110] Next, the participants generate data and insights through group interaction.[111] Accordingly, the researcher should prompt the response of each participant, both the talkative

---

108. Sensing, *Qualitative Research*, 57.
109. Flick, Kardorff, and Steinke, *Qualitative Research*, 142.
110. Sensing, *Qualitative Research*, 36.
111. Sensing, 86.

and the silent ones, since the differences among the participants help gather a variety of opinions. Furthermore, a moderator, a notetaker, and other research team members are recommended. Participants should be reminded to respect the privacy and anonymity of each other after the session.[112]

A one-on-one interview is conducted with individuals to collect the data necessary for research. In qualitative research, the researcher can design semistructured interview questions for each participant. The researcher also requires guidelines and protocols to manage the interview procedure.[113]

Gathering documents is instrumental in qualitative research such as in the evaluative research method. The researcher examines the available public and private documents in order to collect useful information. The researcher has to secure permission from the resource institutions and individuals for a proper use of the available records. These documents can be newspapers, business minutes, letters, personal journals, and other informative articles.[114]

Observation is a supportive tool for gathering data. The researcher pays attention to activities on the research site. Observation requires two levels of recording: descriptive and reflective notes. The researcher ultimately must focus on those elements of observation that contribute to the purpose and theme of the research.[115] John W. Creswell suggests that the interview questions be few and focused.[116]

Summary

In order to explore the need for alternative leadership training models that are culturally contextualized for evangelical church leaders in Ethiopia, I investigated previous research and literature. I gave priority to articles, dissertations, and books written in and about Ethiopia. Then I expanded the circle of literature to examine all of Africa, Asia, Latin America, and the rest of the world. As at the date of my ministry project, I found no journals published in Ethiopia in the area of my research. However, the few graduate-level theses

---

112. Sensing, 120–24.
113. Creswell, *Educational Research*, 226–29.
114. Creswell, 230–31.
115. Creswell, 236.
116. Creswell, 218–19.

available indicated the limitations of the existing formal theological models and the need to consider the culture and setting of the community when designing curricula for theological institutions. The journals written on Africa indicated primarily the limitations of the traditional, formal theological training of the Western models. Furthermore, the articles recommended all the possible resolutions to make leadership training more relevant, experiential, and contextual. Literature written about leadership training in Asia and Latin America indicated that churches in these parts of the world are undergoing a similar struggle of contextualizing their theological training programs. In fact, the literature seems to show that the need for culturally contextualized alternative leadership training is a global concern.

Therefore, the themes in this literature review focused on previous writings and accomplishments regarding developing alternative leadership training models that are culturally contextualized for church leaders in Ethiopia, Africa, Asia, and Latin America. I assessed the past experiences and current trends in training church leaders in Ethiopia. I examined the experiences of churches in Africa in leadership training, both past and present, as discussed by scholars and theologians in and outside Africa. I also examined the strengths and weaknesses of theological education during and after the colonial period in Africa. The need for Bible-based, Jesus-modeled, church-owned, and community-oriented leadership training for churches in Africa is a contemporary cry. The literature written about the past experiences and the present trends in leadership training in Asia and Latin America supports a similar concern and need for relevant, experience-oriented, and cost-effective leadership training models for church leaders.

All in all, the global trend is now to realize the contributions of churches in the Majority World toward making a more relevant and contextualized theology which takes into consideration the existing spiritual, social, political, and economic concerns and needs in the society. Theologians, scholars, and church leaders from around the globe are recommending and encouraging a dialogue leading to the development of a renewed and revised meta-theology as well as local theologies that integrate the holistic concerns and needs among the communities in the respective regions.

CHAPTER 3

Methodology

The problem and purpose of this research is discussed in chapter 1. I will discuss below about the details of the methodology I applied in order to explore elements needed for alternative leadership training models in Ethiopian context.

Research Questions

This ministry project utilized three research questions. The Hiwot Berhan Church of Ethiopia has three levels of leadership – local, regional, and national. The first research question was designed to explore the training elements needed at all levels of leadership in the church. The second question was designed to explore how the anticipated training elements can be sound from biblical and evangelical perspectives. The third research question attempted to discover the methods and means available domestically that enable culturally acceptable and financially sustainable leadership training.

Research Question #1

What are the alternative leadership training elements needed by the leaders in the Hiwot Berhan Church of Ethiopia at the local, regional, and national levels?

This question aimed to explore the need in both the content of leadership training and the delivery method of the training. In order to answer this question, I first applied a specific instrument, namely an interview with focus groups from the Hiwot Berhan Church that reflected various needs of leadership training. In order to answer research question #1, I asked other questions to determine what an ideal Christian leader would look like in the region, how effective the existing formal theological institutions are in producing this ideal leader, what type of alternative training would be needed to produce this kind of leader, what systems and other characteristics could best deliver that content, and what other characteristics unique to the region leaders would need to consider when preparing training for that region. The second tool I designed was a semistructured interview for individual leaders. I asked each leader the same questions designed for the focus groups, but I expected different responses and approaches from the participants in the one-on-one interviews.

Research Question #2

How can these alternative leadership training elements be grounded in evangelical scriptural knowledge?

This question was aimed at discovering the essential training elements in alternative leadership training models for the evangelical churches in Ethiopia, with a specific focus on the Hiwot Berhan Church of Ethiopia. The question sought to ensure that the training elements explored would be grounded in the Scriptures and the evangelical practice and tradition in Ethiopia. I asked each interviewee to identify the cultural and social threats to leadership training, to what biblical and evangelical values Christian leaders should hold, and how these values might be transmitted to emerging leaders. I believe evangelical leaders in Ethiopia need to undergird the evangelical and biblical values of spiritual leadership by identifying some of the harmful cultural, social, and scientific values that can easily penetrate churches and theological institutions. Therefore, both the focus groups and individual participants addressed this question.

Research Question #3

How can a church leadership training program be culturally relevant and financially sustainable in order to meet the long-term leadership needs of the church?

This question aimed to discover the means of delivery for alternative leadership training models that are culturally contextualized for the church. In order to answer this question, I explored some of the domestic resources that are available for the church leadership program. These resources were expected to be sustainable within the specific cultural context. In order to measure the availability of human, financial, and material resources in the country, I conducted an interview with each focus group. I designed one main question and six subquestions to explore the recommendations of the focus groups regarding the sustainability of the leadership training program. The main question I asked was, "What is your recommendation about ways of making the leadership training program relevant, sustainable, and self-supporting?" The six subquestions were as follows:

1. What is the medium of instruction that is preferred by the trainees in your area?
2. What types of national teachers and trainers who can conduct leadership training programs in the vernacular are available in your region?
3. What kinds of leadership training materials are available in the vernacular in your region?
4. What types of training venues and facilities that can accommodate trainees are available in your region?
5. What types of vocational and bivocational trainees are available for the leadership training program in your region?
6. How can the church in this region partner with leadership training programs in financial areas in order to make the training sustainable and self-supporting?

Population and Participants

In this research, I utilized a purposeful sampling and selected four focus groups and four individuals in order to determine the leadership training needs of the Hiwot Berhan Church.[1] The focus groups were homogeneous cultural units, each representing a constituency among which the Hiwot Berhan Church operates throughout the country. The selection criteria for each focus group involved the geographical distribution of the cultural groups throughout Ethiopia, the population size of membership in the Hiwot Berhan churches, and the cultural homogeneity of the group in terms of settlement, language, and shared worldview.

---

1. Creswell, *Educational Research*, 214–15.

The sampling of the individuals in each focus group was based on how well they expressed the training needs of the leadership in the Hiwot Berhan Church. As such, selection criteria for individual members of each focus group involved leaders currently active in the ministry of their respective churches; leaders and congregants well oriented in the history, teaching, and mission of the Hiwot Berhan Church; and leaders and congregants affiliated with the cultural group they represented by speaking its language and sharing its worldview. I selected participants from each cultural region on the basis of these criteria and in consultation with the Research Reflection Team and the National Executive Committee of the Hiwot Berhan Church.

I selected the individuals for the semistructured interview on the basis of two criteria. The first criterion was that they represented the Hiwot Berhan Church's geographical coverage in the country. Therefore, I selected them from four geographical locations in the country: north, east, west, and central Ethiopia. The second criterion was related to their areas of leadership. I selected pastoral leaders, Bible school leaders, and leadership trainers. The participants of my semistructured interviews comprised one individual from each of the four regions I structured for the purpose of this project.

In this study, I selected six representatives for two cultural focus groups and seven for the other two cultural groups, including representatives of full-time (i.e. vocational) leaders, lay (i.e. bivocational) leaders, Bible school administrators or trainers, female leaders, congregants, and youth leaders ministering among the Hiwot Berhan Church of each specific cultural region. I made these selections in the hope that they would prove an adequate and complete group to express the leadership training needs on behalf of their respective regional churches. Table 3.1 sets out the participants of the four focus groups representing the Hiwot Berhan Church of Ethiopia.

Table 3.1 Participants of the Focus Groups

Regions	Types of Representatives	No.
Sidama	Full-time ministers, lay leaders, Bible school administrators, female leaders, youth leaders, congregants	7
Guji-Oromo		6
Amhara		7
Southwestern Ethiopia		6
Total		26

The participants of the individual interviews were pastoral leaders and leadership trainers who came from the Hiwot Berhan Church of Ethiopia located in the different parts of Ethiopia (see table 3.2).

Table 3.2 The Region and Number of Participants in the Individual Interviews

Participants	Ministry	No.
Tigray Region (extreme north)	Pastor	1
Jimma Zone (western Ethiopia)	Pastor and trainer	1
North Shewa Zone (central Ethiopia)	Pastor and trainer	1
Dire Dawa Administrative Council (eastern Ethiopia)	Evangelist and trainer	1

The summary of the population of people groups represented by the cultural focus groups of Hiwot Berhan Church is attached in Appendix A.

Design of the Study

The ministry project underwent the following phases. First, I conducted a group interview with each of the four cultural church groups and an individual interview with the four leaders to collect data; second, I arranged a video recording of each interview session with the four cultural church focus groups and an audio recording of each interview with the four individuals; third, I gathered documents about the history and practice of leadership training in the Hiwot Berhan Church from both public and private owners; fourth, I gathered my field notes with my observations; fifth, I organized the data by transcribing and translating them; sixth, I then started to get an overall understanding of the data by reading it; seventh, I analyzed the data by categorizing it into themes and by labeling the themes with codes; eighth, I coded the text for themes to be used in the research report; ninth, I validated the accuracy of the findings by using member checking and an external audit; and tenth, I presented the first draft to my mentor for his evaluation, recommendations, and input.[2]

---

2. Creswell, 237.

In this qualitative research, I attempted to explore a comparatively better and more relevant training program, namely alternative leadership training models that are culturally contextualized. Furthermore, I chose a qualitative evaluative research method described as "a type of social research that seeks to discover social reality, to probe its capacity for change and to test its boundaries, and on that seeks to change and create social reality."[3] According to Uwe Flick, Ernst von Kardorff, and Ines Steinke, an evaluative method has the following functions: first, the evaluative research method helps to check the effectiveness of a training intervention; second, the outcome of the evaluation research provides support for decision-making and planning in order to control the quality of training anticipated; third, the method is intended to promote, document, and monitor the changes and the learning processes; and fourth, it leads to a deeper understanding of the areas under investigation.[4]

The qualitative evaluative research method has specific advantages that support the type of ministry project I conducted. Some of the unique features of this method are that, first, it is value bound in that it takes into consideration the values of the researcher, the participants, and the community; second, it allows the participants to be involved both in providing the data and in interpreting and confirming the data; third, the evaluation method focuses on the goal of bringing change as a result of communicating the outcome of the research; and fourth, it is flexible in its approach by taking into consideration the diversification of the roles of the participants.[5]

One of the methods encouraged by qualitative evaluative research is "communicative validation." In this method, the participants are invited to check whether their views are properly recorded or not.[6] In my ministry project, I used two validation tools. The first one was to select two representatives from each focus group and review with them the transcription of the focus group interviews in order to receive their approval. The second tool was to select three experts for an external auditing.

The qualitative evaluative research method has certain risks that need to be considered at the time of the presentation of research results. The evaluation

---

3. Flick, Kardorff, and Steinke, *Qualitative Research*, 142.
4. Flick, Kardorff, and Steinke, 137.
5. Flick, Kardorff, and Steinke, 39–40.
6. Flick, Kardorff, and Steinke, 141.

can discover the weaknesses of individuals and/or institutions. The researcher can be caught between being honest to his or her profession and maintaining the confidentiality of the participants. I agree with the recommendation given by Flick, Kardorff, and Steinke: "The presentation of results from evaluation studies can and should be understood as a process of argumentation with participants about the 'issues' in the investigated field."[7] Although the purpose of my research was to explore the need for alternative leadership training models, I found it necessary and enriching to investigate the effectiveness of the existing formal theological institutions that are run by the Hiwot Berhan Church.

The goal of my ministry project in choosing an evaluative method was not to conduct an exhaustive investigation of theological institutions in Ethiopia or even within the Hiwot Berhan Church. Conducting an extensive investigation of the formal theological institutions was beyond the scope of this ministry project. However, I present an evaluative comparison of the existing theological institutions within the Hiwot Berhan Church and the anticipated culturally contextualized leadership training models so that readers of this project will have a knowledge of the background problem in leadership training in Ethiopia that led me to explore alternative leadership training models that are culturally contextualized and applicable to the Hiwot Berhan Church and sister evangelical churches in Ethiopia.

Instrumentation

Interviews and questionnaires represent the methods and tools for collecting data in qualitative research.[8] In this ministry project, my primary instruments to explore the need for alternative leadership training models were interviews with focus groups and individual leaders. I also gathered documents that informed me about the history and practice of the Hiwot Berhan Church in areas of leadership training. I used a field notebook to record my observations as an accompanying tool for the research. Sensing describes the benefits of group interviews: "Through group interaction, data and insights are gathered that are related to a particular theme imposed by a researcher

---

7. Flick, Kardorff, and Steinke, 141.
8. Creswell, *Educational Research*, 213.

and enriched by the group's interactive participative discussion."⁹ A group interview is culturally appropriate in Ethiopia because the participants come from a communal background where decisions are made by consensus.

According to Creswell, focus group interviews are helpful for several reasons. Focus group interviews allow the researcher to collect shared understanding from several individuals and to obtain views from specific people. Furthermore, this type of research facilitates cultural interaction among the interviewees in order to provide accurate information about the need. Since the interviewees in each focus group came from the same church affiliation and cultural group, they cooperated with each other during the process of the interview.[10]

The interview questions were primarily researcher designed. However, the Research Reflection Team contributed a constructive recommendation related to the type and number of questions for the focus group interviews. Three research questions guided the direction of the interviews. Under each main research question, I designed two to six open-ended subquestions. Rose Barbour states, "Focus groups can generate lively discussion and rich data, as participants reformulate their views, engage in debate, and express and explore shared cultural understandings."[11] The guidelines given by Barbour on how to moderate a focus group interview "thoughtfully and attentively in order to maximize the quality of the data generated" helped me greatly:[12]

1. I only attempted to facilitate the discussion; I did not intervene frequently.
2. I was prepared to use prompts or to ask additional questions.
3. I paid close attention to vocabulary used by participants to identify their particular use of the terms "minister" and "leader."
4. I had to frequently rephrase and elaborate the questions so that the participants understood what I expected.
5. I used interim summaries at the end of each research question in order to create a smooth transition from one major theme to the other.

---

9. Sensing, *Qualitative Research*, 120.
10. Creswell, 218.
11. Barbour, *Doing Focus Groups*, 131.
12. Barbour, 131.

6. Even though I had a better knowledge than the participants about some of the themes being discussed, I chose not to act as an expert. I chose to listen to and compliment them.[13]

The time I had with the focus groups was beneficial in three ways. First, I collected an adequate amount of data through the interviews. Second, I was able to perceive the overall leadership situation within the Hiwot Berhan churches, identifying the functional strengths and limitations of the leadership. Third, the discussion created an environment of learning, fellowship, and worship as we interacted with each other.

The second instrument I used in this research was a semistructured, one-on-one interview. I selected four individuals who were pastoral leaders and leadership trainers from four regional settings in the Hiwot Berhan Church. I designed closed-ended and open-ended questions in consultation with the RRT and the expert reviewers. I designed an interview protocol and an interview guideline in the Amharic language to facilitate the gathering of data through one-on-one interviews in order to explore the needed training elements in alternative training models for the evangelical churches in Ethiopia through my evaluative study of the Hiwot Berhan Church. The following guidelines given by Steinar Kuale on conducting interviews were helpful to me during the process of interviewing both the focus group participants and the individual interviewees:

1. An interview for qualitative research is semistructured; it has a sequence of themes to be covered, as well as some prepared questions. However, it is also open to change during the process of interview to make adjustments based on the response of the interviewees.
2. The social interaction created in the interview situation is decisive for the readiness of the interviewee to answer the questions of importance to the interviewer, and for the quality of the answers.
3. Briefing of the subject before the interview and debriefing after the interview will set the stage for the interview.

---

13. Barbour, 114.

4. Preparing two types of scripts for the interview, one in academic language and another in the vernacular of the participants, is a useful approach.
5. The quality of the interview depends on the way the interviewer reacts after an answer is given by a participant. Allowing the interviewee to pause and then to continue an answer, verifying the answers given, and probing for more information is recommended in order to gather the required data.[14]

Kuale's recommendations were helpful and relevant in the process of my research while I was dealing with both focus groups and the individual interviewees.

I was excited and enriched by the views expressed by each participant in both the focus groups and the one-on-one interviews, for the following reasons:

- Each participant was able to express his or her views in a free and independent manner and environment.
- Most of the views in the focus groups were complementary to each other.
- In a few cases, some had views that were extreme, critical, and, at times, conflicting. However, even these views were required to get the full picture of the subject being discussed.
- Redundancy of views that were unhelpful was rare. Almost every participant was excited to express his or her views creatively, adding value to the research.

The third instrument I applied to gather data was collecting and analyzing documents from the Hiwot Berhan Church. Creswell describes documents as follows: "Documents consist of public and private records that qualitative researchers obtain about a site or participants in a study, and they can include newspapers, minutes of meetings, personal journals, and letters."[15] These documents focused mainly on the history and practice of the Hiwot Berhan Church in areas of leadership training. Some of the documents that provided useful information were church business minutes, college catalogues,

---

14. Kuale, *Doing Interviews*, 65.
15. Creswell, *Educational Research*, 223.

graduation yearbooks, anniversary magazines, letters of correspondence between the church and partners, and audio and videotapes. I secured written permission from the national office of the Hiwot Berhan Church of Ethiopia to gather, examine, record, and report the information I required for my research. I used the following procedures to collect the documents:

1. I received a letter of recommendation and cooperation from the denominational office of the Hiwot Berhan Church of Ethiopia.
2. I secured copies of the curricula from the four theological institutions that are owned and operated by the Hiwot Berhan Church. The curricula for Loke Bible School, Pentecostal Theological College, Adola Bible School, and Worancha Bible School are attached in Appendices F-I.
3. I obtained the special edition magazine for the Jubilee anniversary of the church.
4. I received the official list of the regional councils of the Hiwot Berhan Church from the department of evangelism in the denominational office.
5. I referred to a transcribed interview that I recorded twenty years ago while I was serving as the general secretary of the denomination as well as the principal of the Pentecostal Theological College (formerly Pentecostal Training Center). The interview focused on the history of the establishment of the Hiwot Berhan Church and its Bible schools.

The fourth instrument I applied was observation. Michael Angrosino describes observation as "the act of noting a phenomenon, often with instruments, and recording it for scientific purposes."[16] In this research I was a participant observer in that I was involved in the "process of learning through exposure to or involvement in the day-to-day or routine activities of participants in the research setting."[17] I followed the process of observational research as recommended by Angrosino:

1. I selected the research sites;
2. I gained entry into the community;

---

16. Angrosino, *Ethnographic and Observational Research*, 54.
17. Angrosino, 56.

3. I began observing;
4. I took notes of my observations;
5. I identified the discernible patterns in progress; and
6. I gathered helpful principles and patterns that were supportive of my observation.[18]

I had the unique privilege of conducting leadership training and congregational conferences at the research sites simultaneously with the interviews. I met leaders and congregants in large numbers, which gave me an opportunity to talk to them about leadership training needs. I traveled about 2,200 kilometers to the four interview sites – Bahir Dar (Amhara region), Adola (Guji zone), Hawassa (Sidama zone), and Wolayita Sodo (southwest Ethiopia). I conducted five leadership seminars on the Eight Core Values of Christian Leadership designed by the International Leadership Institute (ILI), and that gave me access to 447 leaders. I observed the strengths, weaknesses, opportunities, and threats in areas of leadership development. I gathered written assessments and took summary notes of the views of the leaders and the congregants of the Hiwot Berhan churches.

I travelled to four sites to conduct the focus group interviews. First, I designed an observation protocol with the specific contents that needed to be included in my field notes. I kept a record of my descriptive field notes and reflective observation notes in these places. I finally narrowed down the details of my observations to fit with the purpose of my research in order to help me explore the elements that alternative leadership training models in Ethiopia require.

A pilot test was conducted with a sample focus group in order to obtain feedback on the relevancy of the interview questions. Participants in this sample focus group were representatives from the four cultural groups that came to attend the General Assembly of the Hiwot Berhan Church of Ethiopia.

Expert Review

I obtained an expert review in order to validate the instrumentation because the type and size of the researcher-designed, semistructured interview questions required an expert review. I took four steps to accomplish this task. First,

---

18. Angrosino, 58.

I created the researcher-designed, semistructured interviews. The questions were designed on the basis of the purpose statement, the research questions, and the subjective nature of qualitative research. I selected four individuals as experts to review the instrument and give me feedback. Next, I sent a letter to the experts informing them about the research problem, purpose, and questions. Finally, I created a protocol for the experts so that they could provide their comments regarding the type and size of the interview questions designed for the focus groups and the individual interviews by completing and sending back the form. The elements included in the expert review are given in appendix B.

Variables

The dependent variable in this ministry project had a criterion variable in which the elements needed for alternative leadership training that is culturally contextualized for church leaders were explored. I expected that the project would find the predictor variables for developing these leadership training models. In qualitative research, an independent variable is the element that contributes to the issue of concern, or the dependent variable. The group interviews for the focus groups, the semistructured individual interviews, the documents, and my personal observations and the findings thereafter that influenced the dependent variable represented part of the independent variable. In this specific ministry project, the independent variables were predictor variables required to develop alternative leadership training models for the evangelical leaders in Ethiopia with a focus on the Hiwot Berhan Church of Ethiopia.

Confounding variables can affect and influence the outcome of the dependent variables in this type of research. In the process of exploring the needed training elements, I anticipated the following confounding variables:

1. The phrase and concept "alternative leadership training that is culturally contextualized" might be new and strange to some of the interviewees because most of them were acquainted only with the traditional, formal models of training they experienced in residential Bible schools.
2. The interviewees came from different academic backgrounds. Those from lower educational backgrounds might express training

needs that did not express the actual needs of the churches they represented. During the process of an interview, it is not uncommon for interviewees to say what the interviewer wants to hear instead of the reality on the ground.

3. The participants in each focus group might express distinct leadership training needs of a diverse nature that had no common factor. As a result I might find some of the views of the participants difficult to categorize into a thematic pattern.

Reliability and Validity

In qualitative research, researchers are expected to determine the accuracy or credibility of their findings. According to Creswell, persons conducting qualitative research should apply three forms of validation strategies, namely triangulation, member checking, and external audit.[19] I selected two members from each of the four cultural focus groups to listen to the findings of the research and give their approval. Three external auditors, one with a language background, one with a leadership background, and another with an educational leadership background, read the findings of the research and gave their recommendations and approval.[20]

I repeated the interview for the focus groups four times using similar interview questions, with a total of twenty-six interviewees from different cultural and ministerial settings. The one-on-one interviews allowed me to explore training needs in an in-depth manner. In addition, the documentation on the history and practice of the church provided valuable research elements. Added to all these, my personal observation, sharpened by research skills I had acquired through training and reading, helped me to identify the training elements for church leaders in my nation. Therefore, the research was reliable based on the nature of the instruments applied. I selected the four cultural focus groups and four key leaders from within the Hiwot Berhan Church in consultation with the Research Reflection Team. Furthermore, I also designed the questions for the interviews in consultation with the RRT. I conducted the focus group interviews in the cultural and social settings of the participants. I conducted a pilot test with a sample focus group to check the relevancy of the

---

19. Creswell, *Educational Research*, 259–60.
20. Galvan, *Literature Reviews*, 56.

interview questions. Each focus group was interviewed in Amharic language with a translation into the vernacular whenever needed. The interview sessions for the focus groups were video recorded for proper documentation. The interview sessions with individual leaders were audio recorded. I formed the focus groups in such a way that they geographically covered the national training needs of church leaders in the Hiwot Berhan Church of Ethiopia. I selected group members in such a way that comprehensive information was gathered to address the training needs of church leaders from the perspective of both leaders and congregants. The individuals were selected for one-on-one interviews on the basis of two criteria: first, that they were all leaders in the pastoral, theological, and training areas of the church ministry; second, that they came from four regions in which the Hiwot Berhan Church operated in Ethiopia. Therefore, the validity of the research was high in fulfilling the standard of a qualitative research.

Data Collection

I collected data in the following stages:

1. Securing funds for the project – March–June 2014;
2. Selection of the participants and the interview sites – April 2014;
3. Formation of the four cultural focus groups in the Sidama, Guji-Oromo, Amhara, and southwestern regional Hiwot Berhan churches – April 2014;
4. Organization of the necessary resources for the project – May 2014;
5. Conducting the interviews with the four focus groups – June 2014;
6. Conducting the one-on-one interviews – June 2014;
7. Collection of documents – April–June 2014; and
8. Translation and transcription of the interviews in preparation for data analysis – July 2014.

October–December 2013

This ministry project by its nature required expenses for accomplishment, specifically for transport, participants' per diem expenses, video recording, stationery, translation costs, and honorariums for church executives. To that end, I prepared the budget proposals, requesting donations by writing to partners.

April 2014

Two major events took place during April 2014 in preparation for data collection. First, I selected participants for each cultural focus group and for the individual interviews in consultation with the RRT and the church executive council. I then assigned coordinators from the national office to contact the participants of the focus groups. I contacted the individual interviewees for one-on-one interviews via telephone. I confirmed each participant's agreement to participate in the focus groups through the coordinators. Next, I selected and arranged four interview sites, namely Hawassa (for the Sidama group), Adola (for the Guji-Oromo group), Bahir Dar (for the Amhara group), and Wolayita Sodo (for the southwestern people group, Wolayita, Gamo Gofa, Nyangatom, and Tsamai). The interview location for the individual participants was Addis Ababa, the capital of Ethiopia.

May 2014

During May 2014, as a final preparation for the data collection process, I completed various activities related to organizing the necessary resources, both human and material. First, I selected assistant facilitators and interpreters/translators and provided them with orientation on the purpose of the project and their various duties and ethical obligations in the process of data collection and transcription. Next, I appointed individuals who were responsible for recording the interviews by video camera. I briefed them regarding the purpose of the project and the process of recording. Then I conducted a pilot test of a focus group interview with the cooperation of a few RRT members in order to evaluate the relevancy of the interview questions, and I made the necessary adjustments to some of the questions based on the result of the pilot test. After confirming means of transport to the interview sites, I then confirmed the availability and arrangement of the four interview locations. I sent a copy of the written schedule with the dates of the focus group interviews to the coordinators in order for these to be communicated to each focus group, and I secured final confirmation via telephone.

First Week of June: Interview with Amhara Focus Group

I conducted the Amhara Hiwot Berhan Church focus group interview during the first week of June 2014. I traveled to Bahir Dar, 560 kilometers north of Addis Ababa. The coordinator and the cameraman were from Bahir Dar city. First, I confirmed the arrival of all the focus group participants through the coordinator. Then I visited the venue for the interview and made the necessary seating arrangements. The person doing the video recording arranged his equipment and tested its accuracy. I divided the interview with this focus group into two sessions.

Session 1: Briefing and Orientation (30 Minutes)

In this session, two activities were conducted. First, at the beginning of the session, I briefed the participants and provided orientation. I explained the purpose of the ministry project. The content of the briefing involved sharing the purpose statement, the institution behind the research, what to expect from the research, and the benefits of the ministry project to the Hiwot Berhan Church and the evangelical church of Ethiopia at large.

The second activity was the signing of the informed consent form detailing the ethical responsibilities of both the researcher and the participants. The form was designed in consultation with the Research Reflection Team.

During this first session each participant was encouraged and allowed to ask questions and to express his or her views and concerns about the content and procedure of the interview session, so that I was able to get the best information needed for the research project.

Session 2: Conducting the Interview (2½ Hours)

Four activities took place during this session. The interview was conducted in the vernacular of the cultural focus group (Amharic language). A cameraman video recorded the whole interview session. The accuracy of the video recording was checked. And after the session was complete, the video document was secured and stored for later translation and transcription.

Second Week of June: Interview with Guji-Oromo Focus Group

The focus group interview for the Guji-Oromo Hiwot Berhan Church cultural group occurred during the second week of June 2014. The team, which consisted of the assistant facilitator, an interpreter, a church executive representative, the video team, and me, traveled to Adola, about 450 kilometers south of Addis Ababa. After confirming the arrival of all the focus group participants, I visited the interview venue and made the necessary seating arrangements. The video recording team arranged all their equipment and tested its accuracy. I divided the interview with this focus group into two sessions.

Session 1: Briefing and Orientation (30 Minutes)

In this session, three activities were conducted. First, I gave a briefing and an orientation to the participants. In the briefing I explained the purpose of the ministry project. The content of the briefing included the purpose statement, the institution behind the research, what to expect from the research, and the benefits of the ministry project to the Hiwot Berhan Church and the evangelical church of Ethiopia at large.

The second and central activity was reaching a consensus as to the use of the medium of communication during the interview. All of the participants in the focus group agreed to use Amharic as the medium of communication. The third activity was the signing of the informed consent form detailing the ethical responsibilities of both the researcher and the participants. The form was designed in consultation with the RRT.

During this first session, each participant was encouraged and allowed to ask questions and to express individual views and concerns about the content and procedure of the interview session so that I was able to get the best information needed for the research project.

Session 2: Conducting the Interview (2½ Hours)

Four activities took place during this session. First, the interview was conducted in the Amharic language. Second, a cameraman video recorded the whole process of the interview session. Third, the accuracy of the video recording was checked. Finally, the video document was secured and stored for later translation and transcription.

Third Week of June: Interview with Sidama Focus Group

During the third week of June, I conducted focus group interviews with the Sidama Hiwot Berhan Church cultural focus group. The team consisted of an assistant facilitator, a church executive representative, the video cameraman, and me. The group traveled to Hawassa, 275 kilometers south of Addis Ababa. After confirming the arrival of all the focus group participants, I visited the interview site and made the necessary seating arrangements. The video recording team arranged all their equipment and tested its accuracy. I divided the interview with this focus group into two sessions.

Session 1: Briefing and Orientation (30 Minutes)

This interview session focused upon two main activities. First, I gave a briefing and orientation to the participants. I explained the purpose of the ministry project. The briefing set out the purpose statement, the institution behind the research, what to expect from the research, and the benefits of the ministry project to the Hiwot Berhan Church and the evangelical church of Ethiopia at large.

Second, I invited participants to sign the informed consent form, which contained an explanation of the ethical responsibilities of both the researcher and the participants. The form was designed in consultation with the RRT.

During this first session, I encouraged each participant to ask questions and express individual views and concerns about the content and the procedure of the interview session so I might obtain the information needed for the research project.

Session 2: Conducting the Interview (2½ Hours)

During the second session, I conducted the interview in the Amharic language while interpreting it into Sidamigna for one of the participants. A cameraman recorded the entire interview process and checked the accuracy of the video recording. The video document was secured and stored for later translation and transcription.

Fourth Week of June: Interview with the Focus Group from Southwestern Ethiopia (Wolayita, Gamo Gofa, Nyangatom, and Tsamai)

I conducted the focus group interview for the Hiwot Berhan Church cultural group from southwestern Ethiopia during the fourth week of June 2014. The team, which consisted of the assistant facilitator, a church executive representative, the video team, and me, traveled to Wolayita Sodo, 390 kilometers southwest of Addis Ababa. The arrival of all the focus group participants was confirmed. The venue for the interview was visited and seating arrangements were made. The video recording team arranged all their equipment and tested its accuracy. The interview with this focus group was divided into two sessions.

Session 1: Briefing and Orientation (30 Minutes)

In this session, two activities were conducted. First, the participants were given a briefing and an orientation. I explained the purpose of the ministry project. The content of the briefing included the purpose statement, the institution behind the research, what to expect from the research, and the benefits of the ministry project to the Hiwot Berhan Church and the evangelical churches of Ethiopia at large.

The second activity was the signing of the informed consent form detailing the ethical responsibilities of both the researcher and the participants. The form was designed in consultation with the RRT.

During this first session each participant was encouraged and allowed to ask questions and to express individual views and concerns about the content and the procedure of the interview session so that I was able to get the best information needed for the research project.

Session 2: Conducting the Interview (3 Hours)

I conducted this focus group interview in the Amharic language, the official language through which all four ethnic groups could communicate with each other. A cameraman video recorded the entire interview and checked the accuracy of the video recording. Finally, the video document was secured and stored for later translation and transcription.

I conducted the one-on-one interviews simultaneously with the focus group interviews in the month of June. I invited four leaders from four geographical locations – west, the far north, east, and central Ethiopia – to come to Addis Ababa for the one-hour interview sessions. I briefed each one of them on the purpose of the research. I asked them to sign the consent form and proceeded with the interview in the Amharic language. I recorded each interview session on an audio recorder for later translation and transcription.

July 2014

During July 2014, I conducted various activities in order to prepare for data analysis. First, I listened to the video- and audio-recorded materials in order to get an overview of the data I had collected through the group and individual interviews. Then I translated and transcribed all of the video- and audio-recorded materials from Amharic into English. Next, I read the transcribed material in order to obtain an overall understanding of the views of the focus group participants and the individuals, and confirm the consistency and flow of the content of the material. Then I checked the transcription and arranged the material in preparation for data analysis.

Data Analysis

1. I translated the recorded materials from Amharic into English and then transcribed it. Then I read the material to get an overall sense of it (August 2014).
2. I coded the data by locating text segments and by assigning a code label to them (August 2014).
3. I coded the text for themes to be used in the research report (August 2014).
4. I coded the text for descriptions to be used in the research report (August 2014).
5. The accuracy of the research findings was validated by member checking and external audit (August/September 2014).
6. I presented the first completed draft of the dissertation to my mentor (October 2014).

Ethical Procedures

During the first session of each focus group interview, I issued a written document stating the ethical duties and rights of the participants and myself. Both parties signed the consent form, and I gave the signed form to each participant. The form contained the research title, the voluntary participation of the members of each focus group, the right of each participant to withdraw, the purpose and procedure of the research, the right to ask questions and interact, the benefits and risks expected, the anonymity of each participant in the research report, and the signatures of each participant and myself.[21]

During the data collection phase, the participants of the focus groups were not anonymous, due to the nature of the data collection instrument. However, the identity of the participants in the one-on-one interviews remained confidential. During the data analysis, neither the focus group participants nor the individual participants were named in the transcription. I secured participant approval in writing in advance of the interviews. Copies of the informed consent forms are given in appendixes C and D.

I took several measures in order to protect the confidentiality and dissemination of the data. First, I submitted a written request to the National Executive Council of the Hiwot Berhan Church of Ethiopia to secure their cooperation and written permission. Next, I established a national Research Reflection Team within the Hiwot Berhan Church in order to enhance transparency and accountability during the process of data collection. I sought and received the voluntary participation of each member of the focus groups. Next, I conducted a briefing and orientation session for each focus group before the interview, in which I explained the purpose of the ministry project. Finally, I guaranteed the anonymity of each participant and his or her respective local church in the research report. The transcriptions and the videotapes were accessible only to me.

The participants in the one-on-one interviews were selected on the basis of their resourcefulness and their geographical representation. They came from various cultural and social backgrounds. Their anonymity was secured and the confidentiality of their views was protected. An informed consent form was signed by each of the participants and me.

I made sure to treat all participants equally; participants from lower socioeconomic classes and those with limited academic education received respectful treatment and hospitality during the interview process. I gave each focus group the option to respond in its vernacular out of respect for each ethnic group. However, all the focus groups chose to communicate in Amharic, the official language and a common medium of communication among us. One of the participants in the Sidama focus group chose to speak in his vernacular, which I was able to understand. The travel expenses of all the

---

21. Creswell, 149.

participants were settled, and the research team that included the assistants, the driver, and the video cameraman were paid accordingly. I ensured that I, as well as each participant in the cultural focus groups and in the one-on-one interview group, completed an informed consent form. I secured the data files on my hard drive under password protection. After the study was completed, I destroyed the raw data.

I secured a letter of permit and cooperation from the Hiwot Berhan Church of Ethiopia based on my written request in July 2013. The Research Reflection Team was formed in September 2013. I made budget requests to partners and secured their consent for grant monies in March 2014. By April 2014, I had identified, selected, and confirmed the participants in each of the four cultural focus groups and the four individuals for the one-on-one interviews. The semistructured interview questions that were designed in consultation with the RRT were pilot tested in November 2013. I selected and confirmed the four locations for the focus group interviews. In addition, I arranged the video cameraman who was one of the church staff. All the transport and lodging facilities were arranged for the research team by the month of May. I mobilized the research team to each site that was selected for the focus group interviews in June 2014 in order to collect data through group interviews and store the data by recording it on video. I transcribed, analyzed, and arranged in thematic pattern the data I collected through the four instruments: group interviews, one-on-one interviews, document analysis, and observation. Finally, I coded the data in preparation for reporting the findings of the research to my mentor and, through him, to the research hearing committee.

CHAPTER 4

Findings

The problem and purpose of this research is stated above in chapter 1. I will discuss below about the responses of participants to the research questions designed for the research. The reader will find the details of the problem and purpose of this project in chapter 1.[1]

Participants

Leaders and congregants from the Hiwot Berhan Church of Ethiopia in the Sidama area composed the first focus group. Leaders and congregants from the Hiwot Berhan Church of Ethiopia in the Guji-Oromo constituted the second focus group. Leaders and congregants from the Hiwot Berhan Church of Ethiopia in the Amhara region constituted the third focus group. Finally, leaders and congregants from the Hiwot Berhan Church in southwestern Ethiopia (i.e. Wolayita, Gamo Gofa, Nyangatom, and Tsamai) constituted the fourth focus group.

The total number of participants was thirty. Out of these, eleven were vocational leaders, sixteen were bivocational leaders, and three were congregants. Each focus group had one female leader, and the youths and the congregants were all male. Out of the nine regional states and two administrative councils in the country, four regional states and one administrative council were represented in the focus group and individual interview sessions. The last four interviewees participated in the semistructured interviews (see table 4.1).

---

1. The purpose and problem of the project are discussed in chapter 1.

Table 4.1 Participants and Demographics

Type of Participants	No.	Representation	Regional State	Geographical Distribution
HBC* focus group from Amhara region	7	Pastor, elders (2), trainer, youth, women, & congregant	Amhara	North
HBC focus group for Guji-Oromo area	6	Evangelist, principal, elder, youth, women, & congregant	Oromia	South
HBC focus group from Sidama zone	7	Evangelist, principals (2), elder, youth, women, & congregant	SNNP**	South central
HBC focus group from southwest Ethiopia (Wolayita, Gamo Gofa, Nyangatom, Tsamai)	6	Pastor, evangelists (2), elder, trainer, & women	SNNP	Southwest
HBC leader from Tigray region	1	Pastor	Tigray	Far north
HBC leader from Jimma zone	1	Pastor	Oromia	West
HBC leader from North Shewa zone	1	Pastor	Oromia & Amhara	Central
HBC leader from Dire Dawa Administrative Council	1	Evangelist	Dire Dawa Administrative Council	East

*HBC: Hiwot Berhan Church
**SNNP: Southern nations, nationalities, and peoples

Research Question #1

What are the alternative leadership training elements needed by the Hiwot Berhan Church of Ethiopia at the local, regional, and national levels?

The training elements of alternative church leadership programs needed by the Hiwot Berhan Church leaders were explored. This involved identifying the perspectives of the Hiwot Berhan Church leaders on the ideal church leader, their evaluation of the effectiveness of the existing formal theological institutions owned and operated by the denomination, their recommendations for types of alternative church leadership programs and their delivery systems, and the characteristics unique to their respective regions in relation to church leadership development.

The primary training element explored through focus group and individual interviews was the participants' understanding of the qualities of an ideal church leader in the context of the Hiwot Berhan Church and the specific culture in which it is operating. I first identified the ideal leader and then explored what type of alternative training would be needed to produce that kind of leader. The values the participants held regarding the ideal church leader originated from two sources: cultural community values of a leader and biblical values of a church leader. The community values and the biblical values shared by the participants differed by region. However, interestingly enough, the participants had some community and biblical values that they all shared. According to the cultural community values of the participants, an ideal leader should have the following qualities:

1. Modeling a relationship to God, the family, church, and the community;
2. Being influential and persuasive in speech;
3. Setting an example to the church and the community by managing his or her own family through providing for their basic needs;
4. Being without blame in handling money;
5. Demonstrating peacemaking, conflict-, and problem- resolution both in the church and in the community;
6. Being involved in community events by attending weddings and funerals and by visiting families, such as the sick or those with new babies; and

7. Demonstrating to the congregation an adequate knowledge of the Scriptures and a skill for preaching the Word.

One of the participants from the Sidama focus group made this powerful statement about the role of the church in the community: "In Sidama the church is seen as a peacemaking institution in the community." A participant of the Guji-Oromo focus group emphasized the quality of truthfulness in an ideal leader by sharing the following saying from his community: "One who leads a truthful life will find a ranch full of cattle." The Guji-Oromo are a pastoral, agriculturalist society. The interviewee from the Tigray region expressed the urgency for alternative leadership training:

> Currently, the people of Tigray are earnestly seeking knowledge and information. The production and distribution of training materials in the vernacular through all available media will have a great audience. The youth, especially those in higher education, need to be redeemed urgently. We have to use this window of opportunity for evangelism and discipleship through alternative leadership training.

The response from this individual was an eye opener to me as to the urgency of the task of preparing and publishing training materials for existing as well as emerging evangelical leaders in Tigray as well as in the entire country.

The participants expressed the biblical qualities of an ideal church leader that are desired by the churches in the respective regions. These qualities focused on leading by modeling, managing one's family in a godly way, being financially generous to church ministry, demonstrating a Spirit-filled ministry, preaching and teaching the Scripture in a knowledgeable manner, visiting the sick and the needy, being hospitable, and earning the respect of the outside community by leading a lifestyle that is above reproach.

Tables 4.2 and 4.3 summarize the findings from the focus groups and individual interviewees regarding the biblical and cultural qualities of their ideal church leader.

The second element of alternative leadership training that the participants addressed was evaluating the effectiveness of the existing formal theological institutions that are owned and operated by the Hiwot Berhan Church. The church runs four theological institutions. The Pentecostal Theological College (PTC), founded in 1993, is located in Addis Ababa (the capital city). It grants

Table 4.2 Participants' Responses on the Spiritual Qualities of an Ideal Church Leader in the Context of the Hiwot Berhan Church

Participants	Biblical/Christian Perspectives
HBC focus group from Amhara region	Exemplary in relationship to God, the family, the church, and the community, demonstrates the spiritual and moral qualifications of 1 Timothy 3 & Titus 1, has better knowledge of the Scriptures than the members, endures persecution and hardship, able to teach the Word
HBC focus group from Guji-Oromo area	Demonstrates a spiritual father model, is a person of integrity by keeping his or her word, visits church members in times of need, is a peacemaker and problem-solver, loves, embraces, and nurtures the youth
HBC focus group from Sidama zone	Hospitable, financially generous to church ministries, has previous experience in church leadership, monogamous in marital relationship, available for members in times of need, has good moral standing in the outside community, is a peacemaker
HBC focus group from southwest Ethiopia	Has adequate knowledge of the Bible, has a healthy working relationship with neighboring evangelical churches, manages family well, monogamous in marital relationship, free from alcohol addiction, Spirit-filled, and charismatic
HBC leader from Tigray region	Leads exemplary and godly life, has good knowledge of the Scriptures, is well aquatinted with members
HBC leader from Jimma zone	Holds high moral standards, demonstrates a greater maturity than the members, is diligent in counseling others in the things of God
HBC leader from North Shewa zone	Is a person of prayer, is generous in giving to church work, is able to teach the Word, is passionate about the work of God, demonstrates the fruit of the Spirit
HBC leader from Dire Dawa Administrative Council	Exhibits the spiritual and moral qualifications of 1 Timothy 3 and Titus 1, holds and demonstrates Christian family values, is faithful in handling money, is able to teach, preach, and counsel

Table 4.3 Participants' Responses on the Cultural Qualities of an Ideal Church Leader in the Context of the Hiwot Berhan Church

Participants	Cultural Perspectives
HBC focus group from Amhara region	Able to influence through speech, able to solve problems
HBC focus group from Guji-Oromo area	Influential and attractive, financially stable, faithful in marriage, truthful in handling money, participatory in community events
HBC focus group from Sidama zone	Wealthy and financially stable, takes good care of spouse and children, is persuasive in speech, is a peacemaker, is actively involved in community events
HBC focus group from southwest Ethiopia	Wealthy and financially stable, well educated academically, influential in speech, peacemaking, faithful in handling money
HBC leader from Tigray region	Worthy of respect, influential and persuasive in speech, impacts the community for change, disciplines like a father, has a culturally decent style of dressing
HBC leader from Jimma	Well educated academically, proven in previous leadership experience, decent in behavior, has an attractive personality
HBC leader from North Shewa zone	Gifted speaker and persuasive and charismatic with an attractive personality, wealthy, has proven past leadership experience in the secular realm
HBC leader from Dire Dawa Administrative Council	Is actively engaged in community events, open and welcoming to people, communicative, had a good moral standing even before conversion

a degree in theology and leadership both in the Amharic language and in English. It also grants a diploma of ministry in both languages. The Loke and Worancha Bible schools are located in the Sidama zone, the southern part of Ethiopia. Loke was founded in 1992, and it currently grants a diploma of ministry in English. Worancha is the oldest of all (founded in 1963), and it grants a diploma of ministry in the Amharic language. The Adola Bible School is the newest of all (founded in 1999), and it is a certificate-level institute primarily for church planters. It is located in Guji zone, the southern part of Ethiopia.[2]

The participants' views on the formal theological institutions encompassed the contributions the schools have made to both the trainees and the church and the limitations of the institutions in meeting the needs of the Hiwot Berhan Church. The major contributions of the formal theological institutions of the Hiwot Berhan Church included enabling the trainees to acquire knowledge of the Scriptures, principles of interpretation, and sound Christian doctrine. They also equipped them with the skills of preaching and teaching. Most of the graduates from these institutions became church planters. The graduates of these schools also developed a habit of research and reading that continued into their postgraduation lives. The limitations of the formal theological institutions of the Hiwot Berhan Church included a lack of a clear and distinct mission, the irrelevancy of the curricula for producing leaders, the foreignness of the media of instruction, inaccessibility to the majority of bivocational leaders, a greater focus on intellect than on character formation, the high cost of tuition for the average rural church and individual trainee, an unwelcoming attitude by sending churches after the trainee's graduation, and lack of follow-up and evaluation of alumni in their ministry destinations. One of the participants, who was himself a principal of one of the Bible schools, reported that only three female trainees had attended the school since its establishment. The interviewee from North Shewa zone expressed his concern as follows: "The formal theological institutes of the Hiwot Berhan Church do not have a clear purpose that shows the direction of the trainings. This has resulted in lack of purposefulness in the graduates. The instructors also lack goals that they can align with the courses they are giving."

Table 4.4 summarizes the responses of the participants regarding the level of effectiveness of the formal theological trainings in producing the ideal church leader for the Hiwot Behan churches.

---

2. Hatiya, "Yeethiopia Hiwot Berhan," 27.

Table 4.4 Participants' Responses as to the Effectiveness of Formal Theological Training

Participants	Nearest Institute	Contributions	Limitations
HBC focus group from Amhara region	Pentecostal Theological College	Produced the few existing vocational leaders, developed the interpretive and preaching skills of trainees, helped them acquire knowledge of Scripture and sound doctrine, improved the habit of reading and research, and developed critical thinking	They did not focus on character formation; inaccessible to bivocational leaders; tuition fee was expensive; the curricula were culturally irrelevant; had no follow-up or evaluation of alumni
HBC focus group from Guji-Oromo area	Adola Bible School	The school's presence itself was a witness to the community; it produced church planters, produced the existing effective leaders, improved the preaching skill of trainees; some trainees experienced spiritual transformation	Accessible only to a few (annual intake 20) compared with the size of congregations in the area (300); entrance requirements not established; the curricula lack focus on leadership; the media of instruction is foreign to trainees; not accessible to women; graduates not welcome to pastoral leadership role; tension between trained vocational leaders and the long-standing bivocational leaders
HBC focus group from Sidama zone	Worancha & Loke Bible schools	Produced church planters; some graduates persevered through all obstacles and became effective leaders	Candidates do not qualify as leaders; the institutions are not successful in producing leaders; the curricula do not adequately address contemporary church leadership issues; the curricula are borrowed rather than contextualized; graduates are not given ministry opportunities and financial support; no proper follow-up and evaluation of alumni

HBC focus group from southwest Ethiopia	Loke Bible School	Produced church planters, equipped trainees with the skills of interpretation and preaching	High tuition fee; graduates are not provided with financial support by the churches; some graduates abandoned the ministry due to lack of ministry leadership opportunities in the church and financial support
HBC leader from Tigray	Pentecostal Theological College	It equipped church planters; the ministry-focused diploma program was helpful; it helped the participant discern his or her call and also experience spiritual transformation	The long-cycle time frame separates trainees from their families and congregations; institutions are inaccessible to churches in the region; the institutions did not design accessible models of trainings such as extension programs
HBC leader from Jimma zone	Pentecostal Theological College	The participant graduated from another institution other than Hiwot Berhan	The primary focus is on intellect rather than on spiritual formation; the course contents are foreign and not relevant; the curricula do not help solve existing leadership problems
HBC leader from North Shewa zone	Pentecostal Theological College	Produced very few successful leaders	The mission of the institutions is not clear; the trainees are not purpose driven; they are opportunists; less attention is given to spiritual formation; the annual intake is like a drop in the ocean compared with the size of the churches and the leadership needed in them
HBC leader from Dire Dawa Administrative Council	Pentecostal Theological College	The institutions were not accessible to churches in eastern Ethiopian regions in recent years	The HBC theological institutions are not accessible to churches in the region; the impact of the institutions is insignificant in the region

The third element expressed by the participants was types of alternative church leadership training and the delivery systems required in the Hiwot Berhan Church to produce the ideal church leader. The participants recommended four categories of training to meet the leadership need within the Hiwot Berhan churches. The first recommendation was to reform the existing formal theological institutions. The reform would include designing a clear and distinct mission for each institution, reviewing the curricula and establishing relevant and contextualized course content, establishing a standardized entrance requirement by giving priority to leaders, and introducing new and accessible means of delivering training to bivocational leaders who are serving in both urban and rural settings. This delivery system would be similar to TEE. The second recommendation participants expressed was to pioneer new formal theological institutes in the Tigray region (extreme north), in Bahir Dar (north), in the Jimma zone (west), in Wolayita Sodo (southwest), and in Dire Dawa (east). I propose the following three options in relation to the organization and management of these training sites. First, each site could be an autonomous training center with its own cultural identity expressed and maintained. Alternatively, second, each site could be an extension site for training under the supervision of the national denominational office of HBC. Or, third, each site could be an extension to the existing theological institutions. The participants mentioned two main reasons for the need to establish new theological institutes. First, the existing formal institutions are at a distance, and they are inaccessible for leaders in their regions. Second, the churches in these regions live and serve in different cultural settings from those of the churches where the formal theological institutions are located.

The third recommendation was to introduce short-term leadership training at selected regional centers with the primary purpose of equipping and sending leaders to their respective churches so that they, in turn, might equip the local church leaders. The participants from rural churches who wanted the leadership training programs to be accessible and cost effective for the average bivocational leader in a rural setting recommended this type of training. The fourth type of training recommended by the participants was to encourage local church-based training that would be cost effective and accessible not only to leaders but also to congregants. This type of training would be expected to focus on women's, youth, and children's ministry workers with the goal of discipling them toward Christian maturity and ministry, because these are the groups neglected in church ministries. A female participant from the Sidama area shared her insight about the status of women in the church: "Women are the ones who are mostly exposed to heretical teaching and practices among Sidama Hiwot Berhan churches. They are victims of the immoral practices associated with heresies. In addition, women in this culture are vulnerable to some of the harmful cultural practices such as polygamy." We therefore need alternative leadership training in which women are candidates both for the training and for the role of leadership in the churches at all levels of responsibility.

A participant from the Sidama focus group shared this insightful training objective:

> The Sidama region is evangelistically saturated. Local churches are located almost within walking distance. They are overpopulated with no room for further expansion. Therefore, training in the Sidama region should focus on equipping trainees for cross-cultural and cross-country evangelism and church planting. The churches in the Sidama area should be prepared to mobilize their resources to reach the unreached both in the country and beyond.

Indeed, evangelical churches in Sidama have celebrated their centennial anniversary. These churches need to consider reaching other parts of the nation with the gospel of our Lord Jesus Christ.

Tables 4.5 and 4.6 summarize the types of alternative church leadership training and delivery systems recommended by the participants, both the focus groups and the individual interviewees.

Table 4.5 Types of Alternative Church Leadership Training Recommended by Focus Groups

Participants	Types of Alternative Trainings	Delivery System	Timing
HBC focus group from the Amhara region	Give priority to training of trainers; develop a curriculum relevant to the region; invest in visionary leaders; focus on youth, women, and children's ministry workers; consider local church-based training; consider the size and financial strength of churches; include both urban and rural church leaders; emphasize character formation; consider leaders with low academic levels	Formal theological institute in Bahir Dar city; informal approach for local church-based training	Long-cycle, diploma level program at Bahir Dar city (1–3-month duration for one cycle); short cycle for local church-based training (3–5 days)
HBC focus group from the Guji-Oromo area	Focus on evangelism and leadership; invest in those who have preaching and teaching skills; introduce and develop pastoral leadership; design the mission of the training in consultation with the constituency; focus on youth and women; assume the placement of graduates; emphasize spiritual formation; use the vernacular as the primary medium of instruction; make the training accessible to all types of leaders	The continuity of formal ministerial training at Adola Bible School; informal training for vocational and bivocational leaders at selected regional training centers	Long cycle for vocational leaders; short cycle, seasonal training for the bivocational leaders whose livelihood is pastoral agriculture (September–November, prior to the harvest season)

HBC focus group from the Sidama zone	Primarily focus on training of potential trainers; consider moral and spiritual qualifications as primary entrance requirements; accept mainly those trainees sponsored by churches and not those trainees that are self-sponsored; emphasize practical ministry; give priority to children, youth, and women ministry workers; design centralized but contextualized curriculum on a national level; train to restore helpful cultural values and to confront harmful cultural values; train to refute false teachings and practices prevalent in the region; focus on training incumbent leaders	The continuity of formal ministerial training at Worancha and Loke Bible schools; informal training at regional centers for the majorities of bivocational leaders whose livelihood is agriculture	Long cycle for vocational leaders at the Bible schools; short cycle for the bivocational leaders, the majority of whom have agriculture as their livelihood
HBC focus group from southwest Ethiopia	Focus on emerging and succeeding leaders; design a curriculum on the basis of the academic level of trainees; train with the goal of equipping the whole congregation with discipleship and stewardship; consider the agrarian society with its low literacy rate; design a pre-election training for potential leaders; train to maintain and guide the charismatic movement in the area	Nonresidential formal leadership training at zonal level at Wolayita Sodo town; tutorial method for short-term leadership training aimed at leaders in neighboring towns and villages; informal approach for local church-based training in rural settings	Short-cycle tutorial approach at a zonal center; short-cycle training for local church-based training in rural settings (2–3 days)

Table 4.6 Types of Alternative Church Leadership Training and the Delivery Systems Recommended by Individual Interviewees

Participants	Types of Alternative Trainings	Delivery System	Timing
Tigray region	Establish training venues closer to the ministry sites of trainees; design a contextualized curriculum; establish a strong relationship with sending churches; emphasize the call of God, godly character, leadership, and communication; select a cost-effective and accessible program; focus on developing youth and children as potential leaders of the future	Formal ministerial training for the whole Tigray region at a designated center	Long-cycle training with the training venue located at an accessible distance to churches and trainees
HBC leader from the Jimma zone	Design a contextualized curriculum; focus on practical ministry; train to bring life transformation; train to sharpen the ministry skills of trainees	Formal ministerial training at Jimma center; mentoring by experienced senior leaders; traditional communal counseling by elderly believers	Short-cycle training for both vocational and bivocational leaders who come from the surrounding towns and villages to a designated center for intensive training

HBC leader from North Shewa zone	Establish research-based training; design training at the site where trainees are located; introduce field-based training with close access to churches; train native trainees primarily by native trainers	Informal approach for vocational and bivocational leaders in the local church	Short-cycle training (learning in classroom setting during weekdays and going out for practical ministry during weekends); seasonal, short-cycle trainings during religious and public holidays
HBC leader from Dire Dawa Administrative Council	Establish needs-based training; design culturally relevant training; focus on practical ministry; train primarily local church leaders; address the holistic need of the society through a holistic curriculum	Formal ministerial training	Long-cycle, regular ministerial training to equip leaders adequately

Each focus group and individual interviewee identified characteristics that were unique to their regions that must be considered when preparing local church leaders for those regions. Table 4.7 summarizes the unique characteristics of each region as expressed by the participants.

Table 4.7 Characteristics Unique to Each Region

Participants	Unique Characteristics
HBC focus group from the Amhara region	The theology and tradition of the Ethiopian Orthodox Tewahedo Church is essential as the religious and cultural context of leadership training in this region
HBC focus group from the Guji-Oromo area	The tension between the long-standing bivocational leaders who are the majority and the theologically trained emerging leaders is frustrating the succeeding generation of church leaders
HBC focus group from the Sidama zone	The mushrooming of heretical sects that are abusing the charismatic gifts of the Holy Spirit such as physical healing, prophecy, and the office of apostleship has resulted in both theological deviation and moral deterioration of the churches around
HBC focus group from southwest Ethiopia	The churches in this region broke away from their former denomination and joined the Hiwot Berhan Church as a result of their experience of the charismatic work of the Holy Spirit that was accompanied by speaking in tongues. However, this new experience needs to be grounded in sound biblical teaching in order to channel the ministry of the church in the right direction
HBC leader from the Tigray region	The believers and the society in general are knowledge and information seekers. Therefore, Bible-based teaching and training materials in adequate supply and in multiple delivery systems (physical and electronic) will have a high consumption
HBC leader from the Jimma zone	The history and practice of Islam in Ethiopia needs to be introduced to trainees so that they are able to communicate their message in the religious and cultural context of their recipients

Participants	Unique Characteristics
HBC leader from the North Shewa zone	The selection and appointment of leaders is mainly along ethnic lines. Leadership training in this region must focus on the biblical immersion of the trainees so that biblical values will prevail over and against harmful cultural values
HBC leader from Dire Dawa Administrative Council	This region is the route to the seaport. It is a place where business is booming. The society is multicultural and morally loose. Immorality prevails to the extent of affecting the moral uprightness of believers and leaders. Leadership training is expected to focus on biblical ethics

Research Question #2

How can these alternative leadership training elements be grounded in evangelical scriptural knowledge?

The alternative church leadership training elements that were explored through interviews with focus groups and individuals will be productive only when they are grounded in evangelical, scriptural knowledge. This biblical orientation of the participants was ensured in two ways. First, the participants were asked to identify some of the social and cultural values that are threats to church leadership development. Second, participants were asked to recommend biblical and Christian values that will produce the types of church leaders that are anticipated by the congregations of the Hiwot Berhan Church.

The major social and cultural values that were repeatedly mentioned by participants as threats to church leadership development included the following. First, the low estimation of women and children among many cultures in Ethiopia is a real threat that affects the multiplication of leaders and the process of leadership transition. Ministry to children, young people, and families, specifically women, is a neglected field in the Hiwot Berhan churches. If children, young people, and entire families do not receive adequate ministry and discipleship, the local, regional, and national assemblies of the Hiwot Berhan Church will remain imbalanced in gender and age participation. In addition, the church will not have a succeeding generation of church leaders in the long run. A female participant from the Amhara region expressed her evaluation of the existing training programs and the need for alternative leadership training programs as follows:

> The Pentecostal Theological College used to conduct an extension training program in Bahir Dar some years back. Many other Christian organizations delivered short-term training programs in our city. Several female trainees from our church here in Bahir Dar attended those training programs and earned their diplomas. However, none of these female trainees were equipped to teach and preach the Word. All the training programs emphasized academic achievement. They did not focus either on transforming the character of trainees or on sharpening their ministry skills.
>
> I believe it is essential to assess the cultural values of a community and identify the harmful and the helpful ones before designing a curriculum for training.

Second, the tradition of campaigning for a leadership position and the installment of leaders by vote is a real threat at the local, regional, and national levels. This value is in direct conflict with the biblical value of leadership appointment through prayer, discernment, and the fulfillment of moral and spiritual qualifications. The third threat is ethnocentrism. Ethnic extremism leads to ethnic conflict, which, in turn, will disrupt church unity and activities. The fourth threat is the marginalization and stigmatization of certain professions, such as potters, skinners, and blacksmiths, in some cultures. This harmful practice has destabilized some intertribal marital relationships among believers. Individuals who practice these professions at times are deliberately but silently prevented from obtaining leadership roles. The fifth threat that was expressed by the participants was cultural values related to marriage. The dowry system in some cultures has forced Christian young people either to delay their wedding arrangements or even to abandon them altogether. Arranged marriages between young people have also robbed many couples of their joy and fulfillment in life and ministry. The form of polygyny that is still practiced among some ethnic groups has become a snare to some evangelical leaders whose ministries have come to an end due to this harmful practice.

The focus groups and individual interview participants recommended the following biblical and Christian values to produce the type of ideal leader they need and desire. The basic Christian value recommended was teaching and modeling discipleship in order to produce morally upright, spiritually mature, and relationally healthy church leaders. Related to this value was spiritual formation, which would enable the leader to develop a sound relationship with God, his or her own family, the congregation, and the community. The third biblical and Christian value was Christian marriage and family in which leaders would be instructed in the forming, nurturing, and management of a godly family. The fourth value that participants emphasized was principles of Christian leadership in which leaders would be introduced to the definition, call, selection, appointment, duties, ethics, and transition of leadership. The fifth biblical value that was expressed had to do with the ministry of children, young people, and women. This ministry would be aimed at nurturing them for leadership engagement at the local, regional, and national levels. The sixth value is Christian stewardship. Western missionaries pioneered the church. Since then, the Hiwot Berhan Church has maintained its partnership with both the pioneers and other Western Christian organizations. Although the foreign partners generously granted support with good and godly intentions, on this side of the globe it created a dependent and expectant church. The leaders of the church are expected to teach and practice generosity.

The participants believed that these biblical and Christian values would produce desirable types of leaders if given within the religious and political contexts of the respective churches. Therefore, courses on church and state, the teachings and traditions of the Ethiopian Orthodox Tewahedo Church, the history and practice of Islam in Ethiopia, the living traditional religions in Ethiopia, and contemporary cults and heresies in Ethiopia were highly recommended. Table 4.8 summarizes the responses of the participants concerning the social and cultural values that are threats to church leadership development, and the biblical Christian values they recommend to produce the ideal church leader.

Table 4.8 Social and Cultural Values That Are Threats to Leadership Development and the Biblical Christian Values Recommended by Participants

Participants	Social and Cultural Values as Threats	Recommended Biblical Christian Values
HBC focus group from the Amhara region	Rigidity, lack of flexibility, unforgiving attitude, extreme self-discipline to the extent of self-rejection as an expression of piety, strict control on the youth and the taboo on intimate relationships between opposite sexes, low value of women	Servant leadership, Christian forgiveness, discipleship, the sacredness of marriage, elevating the status of women, children and youth, Trinitarian theology, the tradition and teaching of the Ethiopian Orthodox Tewahedo Church
HBC focus group from the Guji-Oromo area	Low value of women, neglect of younger generations, leadership appointment by vote, traditional marital issues such as polygyny	Developing women, children, and youth ministry, Christian marriage values, pastoral leadership in the local church, principles of biblical leadership for existing and emerging leaders, spiritual gifts, Christian ethics
HBC focus group from the Sidama zone	Campaigning for leadership positions, the revitalization of traditional religions and the claim they are making for regional and national recognition, the marginalization and stigmatization of potters, skinners, blacksmiths, etc., urbanization and the exposure of youth to global modern and postmodern culture	Discipleship, Christian marriage, leadership ethics, sound doctrine, theology of ministry, church-home relationship, biblical doctrine of the human race, the role of women at home, in church, and in the community, children and youth ministry, Christian stewardship, the biblical model of leadership, Bible interpretation and preaching

HBC focus group from southwest Ethiopia	Low economic level of the majority, the mobility of people looking for jobs, local breweries and high alcohol consumption, polygyny	Biblical leadership, the exercise of spiritual gifts, Christian marriage, leadership ethics, cross-cultural evangelism and church planting, church and state relationship, Bible and culture
HBC leader from the Tigray region	The exposure of youth in higher academic institutions to global modern and postmodern culture, the existence of age-long culture that appears to be impenetrable by the strategy of evangelicals to bring transformation	Bible and science (psychology), spiritual formation, mentoring by modeling, the power of the Holy Spirit in the preaching and teaching ministry, the ministry of deliverance from addictions, counseling
HBC leader from the Jimma zone	Leadership considered as a status, leaders abandoning manual tasks after appointment, other church ministries considered humble	Servant leadership, the life of Jesus, Christian love and forgiveness, biblical leadership, the theology of ministry
HBC leader from the North Shewa zone	Leadership sought for its status, aspiring to pastoral leadership as a position, the impact of secular management values, ethnocentrism and appointment of church leaders on the basis of ethnic affiliation, manipulation taken as wisdom	Christian communication, Christian marriage and family, servant leadership, stewardship, the call of God to ministry, passion for evangelism
HBC leader from Dire Dawa Administrative Council	The multicultural and heterogeneous composition of the society and the church's inability to penetrate it and bring transformation	Christian ethics, Christian marriage, survey of Bible books, biblical leadership, the theology of ministry, social sciences, preaching skill

The participants expressed their views on how effective the formal theological institutions of the Hiwot Berhan Church were in producing the ideal Christian leader needed by the churches. The findings indicated limitations among these institutions. At the same time, the participants also recommended biblical values that should be included in an alternative church leadership training program. Table 4.9 compares and contrasts the contents of the curricula of the four Bible schools with the biblical values that should be included in alternative leadership training as recommended by the participants. The findings from the available documents of each institution reveal the limitations of the curricula. First, the curricula of all the institutions either are directly adopted from Western traditions or are translations from the head office. Second, all the institutions have depended on guest instructors who at times preferred courses that fulfilled their own interests rather than the needs of the trainees. Third, three of the institutions do not have standard textbooks in the vernacular and, therefore, depend on personal handouts from the instructors. The findings indicate that none of the four formal theological institutions of the Hiwot Berhan Church has courses on Christian stewardship and spiritual formation.

Research Question #3

How can a church leadership training program be culturally relevant and financially sustainable in order to meet the long-term leadership needs of the church?

Exploring the recommendations of the participants for making the leadership training program relevant, sustainable, and self-supporting was the final element in establishing alternative church leadership training for the Hiwot Berhan Church. Six factors were identified by the participants as means of exploring the relevancy and sustainability of the training: identifying the medium of instruction, the types of national trainers available in the region, the kinds of training materials available in the vernacular, the types of training facilities available in the region, the kinds of potential trainees available in the region, and the ways in which the church in the region might partner with leadership training programs in financial areas in order to make the training sustainable and self-supporting.

Table 4.9 A Comparison between the Existing Curricula and the Recommended Biblical Christian Values

Institution	Academic Level	Discipleship	Marriage & Family	Biblical Leadership	Ministerial Ethics	Stewardship	Spiritual Formation
Pentecostal Theological College	Degree	Two courses	One course	Four courses	One course	None	None
Loke	Diploma	None	None	One course	One course	None	None
Adola	Certificate	None	One course	One course	None	None	None
Worancha	Diploma	One course	Two courses	One course	One course	None	None

According to the participants, the selection of the medium of instruction requires accommodating several languages at the initial stage of the trainings. This recommendation by participants to use more than one language as a medium of instruction originates from the change in the educational policy of Ethiopia. Under the imperial regime, the policy was for Amharic to serve as the medium of instruction in all elementary schools throughout the nation.[3] Students of that era read and wrote in Amharic and in Geez script. However, since 1991 the policy has changed. Currently, instruction in kindergarten and elementary schools is in the mother tongue of the learners.[4] As a result, the churches today have two generations of believers and leaders. The first generation are those who had their elementary education prior to 1991 and, as a result, read and write in Amharic. They cannot read and write in their mother tongue, although they are able to communicate orally in it. The second generation of believers are those who had their kindergarten and elementary education in their mother tongue and, as a result, are able to read and write in it (Amharic and Tigrigna in Geez script and the rest in Latin scripts). According to the participants, an alternative church leadership training program should accommodate the outcome of the two educational policies in its initial stage by identifying a primary and a secondary medium of instruction in order to equip church leaders from both generations.

The second finding for the relevancy and sustainability of alternative leadership training was discovering the availability of the Scriptures in the vernaculars of the people groups the participants represented. Contextualization of the curricula and the training materials is possible only if the trainees have the Scriptures in their vernaculars. Table 4.10 shows the availability of the Scriptures in the languages of the participants I interviewed. This finding is based on the interview I conducted with Dr. Haile Yesus Engdashet, head of the translation department of the Bible Society of Ethiopia, Ato Assefa Lalago, administrator of the Summer Institute of Linguistics in Ethiopia, and Ato Tessema Wachamo, national representative of Word Life, Ethiopia. I conducted the interview with Dr. Haile Yesus face to face on 16 September 2014 at his office in Addis Ababa. The interviews with Ato Assefa and Ato

---

3. G/Ammanuel, *Church and Missions*, 40.
4. Kassaye, "Curriculum Development," 49–80.

Tessema were conducted via telephone and email respectively.[[Set table 4.10 near here]]

Table 4.10 The Availability of the Scriptures in the Languages of the Participants

Languages	New Testament	Old Testament	Whole Bible
Amharic			Available in three versions
Tigrigna			Revised and ready for printing
Guji-Oromo	Available	Translation in progress	Not available
Sidama	Available		At proofreading stage
Wolayita			Available
Gofa	Available		Not available
Nyangatom	Translation in progress		
Tsamai	Translation in progress		

The third finding that was essential for the relevancy and sustainability of the training was discovering the effect of the literacy status of each region. The participants emphatically reminded me that the content of the curriculum and the delivery systems of the leadership training program needed to meet the needs of leaders who are serving in the regions where the literacy rate is low. According to the report by the Central Statistical Agency of Ethiopia in 2007, the literacy rate in Ethiopia was 39.8 percent. Thus, nearly 60 percent of the population of Ethiopia is illiterate. The report also indicated that the male literacy rate was 46.2 percent and the female literacy rate was 33.3 percent. In contemporary Ethiopia, educational institutions, facilities, and opportunities are more accessible in urban areas than in rural areas. Therefore, I assume that the literacy rate is higher in urban areas than in rural areas. However, I cannot verify this assumption at present. The sustainability of the alternative church leadership training program depends on the literacy of the trainees. Table 4.11 shows the literacy rate in the participants' areas.

Table 4.11 Population Five Years Old and Above by Literacy, 2007

Participants	All Persons	Literate Persons	% Literate
Amhara	14,884,877	5,651,835	38.0
Tigray	3,686,232	1,673,427	45.4
Sidama zone	2,488,781	1,069,574	43.0
Wolayita zone	1,281,565	590,545	46.1
South Omo zone (where Nyangatom is located)	473,118	101,188	21.4
Gamo Gofa zone	1,329,805	451,466	33.9
Guji zone	1,117,147	367,316	32.9
Jimma zone	2,064,650	669,853	32.4
North Shewa zone (Oromia region)	1,226,919	369,851	30.1
Jimma special zone (the city of Jimma)	110,758	92,849	83.8
Hawassa city administrative zone	233,039	175,746	75.4
Ilu Aba Bora zone	1,073,578	446,336	41.6

The finding on the types of national trainers available in the region indicates that three types of potential trainers are available. First, most of the regions from which the participants came have vocational leaders who have completed formal theological trainings and are qualified to teach. Second, some bivocational leaders also have completed formal theological trainings and are available to teach. Third, churches in the area have vocational and bivocational leaders in other evangelical denominations who have completed formal theological training and are ready to partner with the alternative church leadership training program that the Hiwot Berhan Church intends to conduct.

As for the kinds of training venues and facilities that are available for alternative leadership training, the participants identified three types. First, the existing Bible schools are available for both formal and informal trainings when their regular classes are not in session. Second, most of the local church buildings have classrooms and sanctuaries that are available during weekdays for short-cycle trainings. Third, rental guesthouses that are owned by other evangelical denominations are available for short-term trainings.

The greatest challenge for alternative leadership training, according to the findings based on the reports by the participants, is the lack of training materials in the vernaculars of each region. A few training materials are available in English. Some training materials are also available in Amharic. The availability of training materials in the vernaculars spoken by the people groups the participants represented is negligible. The challenge is both in the relevancy of the existing materials and in the amount of materials required in light of the biblical Christian values the participants recommended.

The last finding concerned ways in which churches in each region could partner with the leadership training program in financial areas in order to make the training sustainable and self-supporting. The finding shows both the potential the churches have for a self-supporting training and the limitations with which they are struggling. The participants affirmed that all the potential trainees from all churches of the Hiwot Berhan denomination could afford to purchase the training materials if they were prepared and presented in their vernaculars. Second, bivocational leaders serving in urban churches could sponsor themselves for both the formal and the informal types of alternative leadership training. All the local churches in rural settings are committed to offer their local church buildings and their homes to host short-term leadership trainings.

However, the findings indicate that the financial sustainability of the alternative leadership program has three challenges. First, the Western pioneering missionaries fully sponsored both long-cycle and short-cycle leadership trainings in the past. The Hiwot Berhan churches have developed dependency on foreign aid for over half a century. Second, other Christian organizations from within the country and from outside have spoiled the churches by heavily subsidizing both formal and informal theological trainings. Third, Hiwot Berhan churches that are planting new churches have no time limit as to how long they will continue supporting the new churches financially. The newly planted churches go on enjoying the free manna distributed by a mother church and, as a result, are robbed of the privilege and blessings of tasting the fruit of the land that is achieved through the grace of giving. All the sponsoring groups have the godly intention of supporting the financially struggling churches. However, all the groups who are sponsoring leadership training would have done better if they had equipped these leaders with the knowledge and skills of Christian stewardship. The participants stated that the training of trainers in each region would still require outside support in terms of money, training materials, and the trainers themselves. One of the participants in the focus group from the Amhara region made this statement about financial sustainability:

> The key to financial sustainability lies not in the trainers or the leadership of the churches. The congregation is the key to the financial sustainability of all the church's ministries. God's resources are God's people. The task of the leadership is teaching Christian stewardship to their respective congregations, setting the example in practicing generous giving, and being transparent and accountable in managing God's resources in the church. The financial success of the alternative leadership trainings can be attained by mobilizing our congregations for generous giving and for demonstration of financial stewardship in every aspect of church ministries.

The leaders of the Hiwot Berhan Church are expected to mobilize their congregations by involving them in the ministry of Christian stewardship so that both the church and the stewards reap the blessings of generosity.

Appendix J presents a summary table of the findings explored among the participants about ways the churches in the different regions can partner with the alternative leadership program in financial areas in order to make the training program sustainable and self-supporting. The participants expressed their readiness to provide facilities, to host trainees in their homes, and to purchase training materials.

The findings of this research agree with the biblical and theological foundation that is discussed in the literature review, namely Jesus's example of training the Twelve as seen in Mark 3:13–19, in the following areas. First, most of the participants recommended that the alternative leadership training programs give priority to character formation instead of academic achievement. This recommendation is in perfect agreement with the fact that Jesus's primary purpose in choosing the twelve disciples was that they might stay with him with the goal of imitating his lifestyle (Mark 3:14). Second, the participants in this research proposed that the alternative leadership trainings be types of in-service trainings in which developing the ministry skills of the trainees would be considered part of the curriculum. This is also in agreement with Jesus's pattern of training in which he called the twelve apostles for the ministry of preaching and deliverance (Mark 3:14–15).

    Third, the participants expressed their concern about the types of trainees sent to the formal theological institutions and the admission criteria applied. Jesus's selection of his disciples through prayer is an important principle that all training program developers must practice. Establishing a training purpose, designing the qualifications of candidates, praying for divine guidance, and conducting face-to-face interviews for discernment are principles learned from Jesus. Fourth, the participants in this research expressed their concern that the trainees for alternative leadership training programs would need to have a passion for evangelism, missions, and the multiplication of new churches into areas that have not yet been reached with the gospel. This is in agreement with Jesus's goal in calling and training the twelve disciples. Jesus said to his first disciples, "Come, follow me . . . and I will send you out to fish for people" (Mark 1:17). The recommendations given by the participants regarding the selection criteria of trainees, the purpose of trainings, the delivery systems, and the sustainability of training programs are grounded in the timeless principles of Jesus's pattern of choosing and training the twelve apostles in Mark 3:13–19 and parallel passages in the gospels.

Summary of Major Findings

I had the privilege of observing the leadership situation in different locations and culture groups. I talked to as many leaders as possible to assess the leadership training needs. I also gathered written feedback from the participants who attended the trainings, which helped me gather as many facts as possible concerning the training needs of the leadership in the Hiwot Berhan Church. I examined four types of documents that were helpful for enriching my research with supportive data. The documents were the curricula of the formal theological institutions of the Hiwot Berhan Church, a special edition of the magazine published for the jubilee anniversary of the Hiwot Berhan Church, the 2007 Population Census Report by the Central Statistical Agency of Ethiopia, and books and journals authored by Ethiopian and other African writers. The following is a summary of the major findings of this research on the elements of alternative church leadership training:

1. Identifying the ideal church leader within a specific cultural setting will help to determine the content and the delivery system of leadership training;
2. Evaluating the effectiveness of the existing formal theological institutions in producing the already identified ideal church leader is helpful for determining the direction of an alternative training program;
3. An assessment of the elements needed for an alternative leadership training program will help in designing the content of the training and selecting the delivery system that is relevant;
4. The social and cultural values that are threats to developing leaders and the biblical Christian values to which leaders need to hold are foundations upon which an alternative leadership program should be established;
5. An alternative leadership training program seeks ways to make the program culturally relevant and financially self-supporting and sustainable.

CHAPTER 5

Discussion

Major Findings

I discovered five major findings in the process of this research that are essential elements for alternative church leadership training.

Identifying the Ideal Church Leader within a Specific Cultural Setting

Every people group has community values about certain professions and practices such as leadership. The participants from diverse cultural groups who were working under the same denominational umbrella of the Hiwot Berhan Church of Ethiopia held to some helpful community values about an ideal leader. Prior to my research, I had observed two major qualifications based on community values that churches in rural areas expected from their leaders. These were an exemplary marital relationship and hospitality. However, during the interviews, I discovered that financial stability and persuasiveness in speech were the leading qualities from a cultural perspective that churches expected from leadership candidates. Among these communities that the participants represented, a leader is first expected to follow a fatherhood model, being one who rebukes the young, who mediates between conflicting groups and individuals, and who solves community problems. Second, a leader in these communities is expected to demonstrate the ability to persuade and influence others through speech. Third, a leader also must have financial stability in order to meet the needs of his or her own family before even attempting to lead a wider community. The most outstanding biblical perspective on the ideal church leader that I observed in these Christian and cultural groups is that a church leader is expected to be a spiritual model to followers in matters of moral integrity, social relationships, and financial management. Failure in these matters is failure in the leadership role. Demonstrating scriptural knowledge and the skill of preaching are not considered by the participants to be an end in themselves; they are means to an end, which is the formation of leadership character.

In this research I discovered that the participants described the qualities of the ideal church leader from their cultural and biblical perspectives. The primary quality of the ideal leader is character-related, in that the leader exhibits godliness by setting an example to followers in the areas of relationship to God, the family, the congregation, and the community. The skillfulness of the leader in speech, in the ability to preach and to administer, and in solving problems was also emphasized by the participants. The literature review in this research supports the findings in the following ways. First, the literature established that the formal theological training found in Ethiopia and other Majority World countries that is designed on the Western model neglects the cultural values and traditions held by the community. Second, the literature also supports the finding that character formation was the primary qualification that the leadership in the Hiwot Berhan Church anticipated from the ideal church leader.

In the training of the Twelve, one of Jesus's purposes was to have the disciples with him. This call for intimacy, imitation, and identification had the ultimate goal of spiritual transformation in the character of the apostles. An ideal Christian leader according to Jesus is one who imitates the Master as a disciple (Matt 10:24–25). Lemma Degefa describes the call to leadership in simple yet emphatic terms: "The primary call of a leader is following Jesus Christ. . . . When God calls a person to him, it is for the purpose of shaping the person and working through that person. He does not call a person to be a spectator."[1] Even the opponents and persecutors of the early church witnessed that the mark of true discipleship and leadership was demonstrating Christlikeness in one's lifestyle and ministry (Acts 4:13).

---

1. Degefa, *Yehiwot Wuquir*, 104, 115.

This finding about the ideal church leader within a specific cultural setting will inform my personal ministry and the ministry of the Hiwot Berhan Church in several ways. First, identifying believers' cultural and biblical perspectives on the ideal church leader is essential for the process of leadership selection, development, and appointment. Second, hearing the cultural perspectives of the participants on an ideal leader was an eye-opening experience that brought me to a conviction to preserve helpful community values, such as managing the family by polishing these cultural values with scriptural principles. Third, a long-term task awaits individual leaders and churches in developing the biblical evangelical values of believers and leaders regarding the identity, character, and ministry of an ideal church leader.

Fourth, this finding concerning the qualities of an ideal church leader will bring a transformation to the outlook of both leaders and congregants in the Hiwot Berhan Church in their aspiration for the role of leadership and in facilitating the selection of leaders. According to the *Revised Constitution of the Ethiopian Hiwot Berhan Church* of 2013, almost every local church has a team of bivocational leaders called elders who are elected to office for a three-year term (Article 45.5). These elders hold their duties and responsibilities as a corporate entity. This research informs the denomination to consider two amendments in the composition of local church leadership. First, the members of the local church leadership team need to demonstrate a gift-based individual identity in addition to the corporate identity they hold as a team. I recommend that the team members represent the ministries in the local church, such as the children's ministry, youth ministry, and family (women's) ministry. Second, it is highly recommended that pastoral leadership be introduced in every congregation, with each church installing full-time and theologically trained pastors who are able to care for the congregation and train, mentor, and guide the bivocational leaders.

The fifth way that this finding informs the church is through formal and informal leadership training programs in the Hiwot Berhan Church inculcating the qualities of an ideal church leader in their entrance requirements and curricula. Sixth, I have learned two lessons about the place of cultural values. First, I should not impose values that are foreign to churches which live and serve in their specific indigenous culture. Second, I should not impose a teaching that will eradicate the communities' helpful cultural values.

The Effectiveness of Formal Theological Institutions in Producing the Ideal Church Leader

Prior to my research I had closely observed the formal theological institutions of the Hiwot Berhan Church. I knew that the two main areas of emphasis in their curricula are biblical knowledge, and evangelism and church planting. I had also witnessed that some of the successful incumbent leaders at both the local and the national level were initially the products of these formal institutions. However, the relevancy of their curricula, the media of instruction, their accessibility to bivocational leaders of rural churches, and the relationship between the institutions and the churches have been my continuous concern. During the interviews I held with the focus groups and individuals, I discovered that the participants had a balanced view of the contributions and limitations of these institutions. Transferring biblical knowledge, equipping trainees with interpretive and preaching skills, and empowering students for evangelism and church planting were the major contributions of the institutions expressed by the participants.

One major finding from the interviews was that the limitations of the formal theological institutions of the Hiwot Berhan Church outweighed the contributions they have made. Three of the four Bible schools have existed for over twenty years. The limitations listed by the participants included lack of clear mission statements, the irrelevance and foreignness of the curricula to producing ideal church leaders, the media of instruction being foreign to trainees, inaccessibility of the programs to the majority of leaders, especially to bivocational leaders in rural churches, and the high tuition fees that are not affordable by the average rural church leader.

Another observation from the interviews was the strange use of the words "leaders" and "ministers" (*meri* and *agelgai* in Amharic) by most participants. In their understanding and context, "leaders" were those bivocational leaders who served as elders and deacons in the local church. "Ministers" were the evangelists, pastors, teachers, and other ordained and full-time staff in the local church. This dichotomy implies that "ministers" are not considered "leaders" in the context of the participants' churches. A leader is associated with the task of administration. Believers understand "administration" or "leadership" according to its secular values in which it is considered as identical with managing employees, finance, and property. Therefore, they do not expect pastors, evangelists, and other ministers to be involved in such professional and secular tasks. However, the elders of the church, who are bivocational and have experience in secular management, are expected to handle such professional tasks in the church. The intention is to protect the *spirituality* of ministers. However, they hold to this practice out of scriptural ignorance. Ministers are called to lead congregations. Ephesians 4:7–16 lists gifts implied for leadership given "to equip [God's] people for works of service" (v. 12). The passages 1 Timothy 5:17, Hebrews 13:7 and 17, and 1 Peter 5:2–4 all imply that ministers serve their people both in leading and feeding them the word of God. Leadership in the biblical understanding is not a necessary evil that ministers must avoid or try to escape. It is rather a gift of the Holy Spirit like any of the other supernatural gifts (Rom 12:8; 1 Cor 12:28).

After going through the data I collected, I discovered a major finding related to the decline of these formal theological institutions in producing the types of leaders anticipated by the Hiwot Berhan churches. The officers of the theological institutions admitted that the number of new applicants from the Hiwot Berhan Church has greatly declined. The Bible school at Loke even had to close down for a year due to lack of applicants. The formal theological institutions did not establish strong relationships with the churches prior to the selection of trainees, during the training, and after the trainees had completed their training. The churches did not know the mission for which these institutions existed. The institutions did not promote their mission among the churches. As a result, the institutions did not have a belongingness with the churches, and the church leaders acted as if they did not own these institutions. This misunderstanding between the college officers and church leaders has led to the theological institutions becoming homes for self-sponsored and self-initiated trainees who are not indebted to the church and its leadership.

The literature in this research fully supports the findings about the contributions and limitations of the formal theological institutions of the Hiwot Berhan Church. The Western missionaries who were the early pioneers of most of the higher theological institutions in Ethiopia contributed to both the church and the community through transmitting biblical knowledge, preaching skill, and a holistic approach to community outreach. However, the curricula in the formal theological institutions were irrelevant to most cultures. They were not accessible to the majority of people in rural settings. The media of instruction were foreign to the trainees. The tuition fees were high, and the training programs were not financially sustainable and self-supporting.

In the biblical theological framework of this research, I established two facts. First, the master-disciple model of training that Jesus applied is a timeless principle that churches of every generation functioning in all geographical and cultural settings have to consider. Training is effective when knowledge, skill, and character are imparted through modeling. Jesus accomplished training that focused on character formation and a transfer of skills; therefore, that is the model contemporary churches need to anticipate.

Second, Jesus's model of training the Twelve is timeless because it was a purposeful training. Jesus clearly stated his purpose right from the beginning. He equipped his disciples to preach the good news and to cast out demons. The leadership of both the Hiwot Berhan Church and the formal theological institutions will benefit if they learn from Jesus. They need to establish a clear and relevant mission for each institution. They need to ensure that the curricula, the teaching materials, and the delivery systems are all aligned with the one clear purpose for which each institution exists. Jesus taught, practiced, and demonstrated his purpose and then commissioned the Twelve to implement that purpose which they had learned and practiced. The contents of his training and the delivery systems he applied were in perfect alignment with his intended purpose.

This finding will help the leadership of the Hiwot Berhan Church and the officers of the formal theological institutions to initiate a reform in the areas of reviewing the mission of each institution, in redesigning the curricula of all the institutions, in reestablishing the entrance requirements of trainees, and in building sustainable relationships between the churches and the Bible schools.

Elements Needed for Alternative Church Leadership Training Programs

I have ministered in and through the Hiwot Berhan Church for forty-two years. I have served in several leadership roles, such as trainer, principal of a Bible school, and general secretary of the denomination. Prior to my research, I had observed the need for short-term leadership training with a contextualized curriculum that would be accessible to bivocational leaders in rural churches. I envisioned a training that would use vernaculars as the media of instruction, supported by training materials written in the vernaculars, and with a tuition fee affordable by the average rural minister.

However, during the interviews, I gained new insights that broadened my horizons concerning the available options in alternative church leadership training. I observed four leadership training options for the Hiwot Berhan Church. First was the need for the continuity of the existing formal theological institutions but with major reform in the areas of their mission, curricula content, and delivery systems. Mentoring, tutorial, and field-based practical ministry were recommended as additional delivery systems to the existing lecture. Participants recommended that all formal theological institutions train both church leaders and church planters to witness a balanced church growth in spiritual, numerical, and geographical dimensions.

The second observation was the need to establish new formal leadership training programs in Wolayita Sodo (southwest), Bahir Dar (north), Tigray (far north), Jimma (west), and Dire Dawa (east). The need for relevant and sustainable formal leadership training in these locations is apparent for two reasons. First, the Hiwot Berhan churches in these areas do not have easy access to the existing formal theological institutions. Second, all except the churches in the Wolayita area are serving among the least evangelized peoples in the country.[2] The time frame recommended for these trainings is short cycle, and the preferred delivery systems are mentoring, tutorial, communal consultation with senior leaders, and field-based practical ministries. The training would appeal to both vocational and bivocational leaders serving in urban and rural settings.

The third observation was the need for short-term leadership training at selected regional and zonal centers in which trainers would make up the target group. Potential trainers available in the regions and who can communicate in the vernaculars would be equipped in short-cycle trainings so that they, in turn, can go back to local churches to develop leaders of various ministries there. The potential trainers would be both vocational and bivocational who are available to offer their time, skills, and even resources to develop the leadership of the local churches. This type of alternative leadership training seems to be the most appealing given the leadership needs of the Hiwot Berhan Church, for two reasons. First, the majority of the members

---

2. Degefa, 269.

of the local church leadership teams are bivocational leaders who are elected to the office of eldership for a three-year term. Second, the statistical data of the current status of the church supports this type of leadership training. According to data published in 2010, the Hiwot Berhan Church denomination had about two thousand local churches that were organized into twenty-six regional councils. In addition, the denomination had about six hundred outreach stations that were growing to be local churches. The population of the church was estimated to be 1.7 million. The number of full-time vocational ministers was estimated to be two thousand, of which 450 were short-term church planters sent to various unreached people groups.[3] According to a recent report by the chairman of the board, the population of the church is now about two million. The regional councils have reached fifty. Assuming that each local church has an average of five members in its leadership team, the Hiwot Berhan Church has a total of ten thousand bivocational leaders who are potential trainees for the alternative leadership training program. Therefore, I conclude that the most appealing type of alternative leadership training for this majority of leaders is the short-term training that is accessible and cost effective.

The fourth training dimension I discovered through the interviews was the need to create local church-based leadership training. The primary purpose of such training would be to equip bivocational church leaders who serve in rural areas where the literacy rate is low, and those who cannot afford to travel to regional training centers. The second purpose of such training would be to equip local church workers ministering to children, the youth, and women so that they can prepare these groups for leadership in the near and distant future. The third reason given by participants is that training the whole congregation for discipleship and stewardship is foundational to overcome the spiritual immaturity prevalent among the churches.

I made one major observation about the delivery system that is fitting for leadership training. Church leadership is a spiritual gift. It is a divine wisdom imparted by God through the Holy Spirit (Rom 12:8; 1 Cor 12:27–31; Eph 4:7–16). Leadership is a skill in which the person demonstrates talent by discharging his or her duties through managing God's resources – human, material, and financial. Therefore, leadership training requires focusing on

---

3. Hatiya, "Yeethiopia Hiwot Berhan," 28.

the impartation and development of leadership skills through the content of the courses and the types of delivery systems applied. The biblical narrative on the construction of the tabernacle as recorded on Exodus 36 is a relevant illustration for my finding:

> "So Bezalel, Oholiab and every skilled person to whom the LORD has given skill and ability to know how to carry out all the work of constructing the sanctuary are to do the work just as the LORD has commanded."
>
> Then Moses summoned Bezalel and Oholiab and every skilled person to whom the LORD had given ability and who was willing to come and do the work. (Exod 36:1–2)

This text implies three types of skillful workers, as shown in table 5.1.

Table 5.1 Types of Skilled Workers in the Tabernacle

Type 1: Bezalel & Oholiab	Type 2: Skilled Workers	Type 3: Willing Workers
Designers	Skilled assistants working under type 1	Volunteers
Doers	Volunteers	Doers of multiple tasks such as stewardship of resources
Trainers	Trainees	Working under supervision
Supervisors	Protégés	

In the alternative leadership training program recommended for the Hiwot Berhan Church, I observe that the following skills need to be included in the curriculum:

- How to minister the Word (the skill of preaching and teaching);
- How to evangelize and plant churches (the skills of conducting surveys, witnessing for Christ, discipling new converts, baptizing in water, establishing and leading a local church);
- How to nurture new converts (the skills of mentoring, counseling, praying, training);
- How to lead a congregation (the skills of leading worship, music, keeping records, serving the Lord's Table, managing human, material, and financial resources, organizational leadership);

- How to develop leaders (the skills of training, writing training materials, communication, administering training institutes).

I recommend the following delivery systems to communicate the courses:

- Select and appoint trainers who have ministry leadership experience in local church settings;
- Invite senior ministers to come and share their leadership experience;
- Arrange trips to ministry fields;
- Use the traditional consultation and consensus method to learn from each other in an informal and intimate way;
- Assign trainees to minister for a short term under the supervision of selected and exemplary senior leaders;
- Design the courses in such a way that the instructional method includes practical ministry both in classroom interaction and in the assignments to be done outside class.

The literature in this research fully supports these findings on the need for alternative church leadership training. First, both the literature and the findings establish that a reform, not a removal, of the existing formal theological institutions is required. Second, the multiplication of formal leadership training institutions that have a clear purpose, relevant curricula, and contextualized delivery systems is highly recommended in both the literature and the findings. Third, innovative training models that take into account the type of anticipated ideal leader, the media of instruction, the relevancy of the delivery systems, the literacy rate of the society, the accessibility of the training to both vocational and bivocational leaders, and the cost effectiveness and financial sustainability of the program are recommended in the literature as well as in the findings.

The Swedish Pentecostal Church Mission, which was the pioneer of the Hiwot Berhan Church, started working in Ethiopia in 1962 by establishing a vocational and technical training center at Hawassa. Parallel to this event, they introduced a leadership training program for all evangelical denominations and Christian university students. The training was conducted for three weeks during the Ethiopian rainy season (August). This short-term training continued until the rise of the Communist regime (1974–91). The duration of the training was then reduced to one week. This short-term leadership training program was later introduced in Wondo Genet, Worancha, Addis Ababa, and Jimma areas. The mission also established a one-year Bible school at Hawassa for church planters who were mostly recruited from rural churches.[4] Thus the findings of this research are supported by the documents in the Hiwot Berhan Church archives. The implication is that the church needs to renew its leadership training programs by embracing both long-cycle formal leadership training programs and short-cycle nonformal leadership development models to produce the types of leaders the churches need.

In the theological framework for this research, Jesus's model of training the Twelve, we see that Jesus's training of the disciples was primarily through instruction on-site. It was heavily field-based training in which Jesus sent out the Twelve on a short-term practice mission followed by evaluation, correction, and recommendation. Second, the approach Jesus used and that his followers later applied was informal training in which followers learned through real-life situations as well as through intensive instruction within local church settings. The formal and informal training in the early church required an exemplary mentor whose life and ministry was a model.

The findings on alternative church leadership training inform the Hiwot Berhan Church leadership to consider the following transformations. First, the church needs to conduct a thorough evaluation of the formal theological institutions regarding the purpose for which they exist, their curricula, the media of instruction, the qualification of trainees, the delivery systems, the tuition fees, and the destinations of the alumni. Second, the church needs to assess the location and distribution of the existing formal theological training and consider ways of extending the training programs into areas that are not currently benefiting from these formal theological institutions. Third, Hiwot Berhan Church leaders are also expected to listen to the recommendations of local leaders in rural settings whose vocation, financial status, and literacy rate demand an alternative leadership training that fits their situation. It is now time for Hiwot Berhan Church leaders to reflect on the training models of pioneering missionaries in the past in that conducting formal theological trainings and informal leadership development programs simultaneously might be beneficial to the vocational and bivocational leaders of the Hiwot Berhan Church.

---

4. Hatiya, 13, 22–23.

The Social and Cultural Values That Are Threats to Developing Leaders and the Biblical Christian Values to Which Leaders Need to Hold

Prior to my research, the three social and cultural values that I had observed as threats to leadership development were the secular status syndrome from the world of management, the cultural marital practice of polygyny, and the cultural value of decision-making by communal consensus, which prevents individual gifts and skills from shining out. However, during the focus group and individual interviews, I discovered other contemporary social and cultural values that are threats to leadership development. The primary threat is the political value of electing leaders by vote. This practice has two dangers. First, leadership candidates campaign for election in the same manner that political leaders campaign for political office. Such a campaign involves undermining the reputations of competing candidates, using superficial, manipulative language, investing large sums of money to buy votes, and recruiting blood relatives and close friends as promoters of the election campaign. Second, Ethiopia is a multiethnic country. The urban, regional, and national assemblies of the Hiwot Berhan Church have a multiethnic composition. The probability that voters will cast their ballots along ethnic lines is high. As a result, this political value of electing leaders by vote has caused contention and strife among leadership candidates. It has several times resulted in disruption and division within the denomination.

The second cultural value that is a threat to leadership development is a global cultural value rather than a local one. It is the impact that modernism, postmodernism, and globalization have on the youth in urban churches and on those in higher educational institutions. Drug addiction, alcoholism, and perverse types of sexual sins are some of the moral threats that are dragging the youth away from pursuing godliness and a passion for ministry. The Hiwot Berhan Church leaders working in Mekelle (Tigray), Bahir Dar (Amhara), Jimma, Hawassa (south), and Dire Dawa have sensed this threat as they work closely among the youth in the universities located in their respective cities. The *Nazarene* magazine is one of the voices of Christian university students and alumni in Ethiopia. One of the objectives of this magazine is as follows: "To identify the teachings and philosophies that are transmitted through entertainment programs from abroad, practices which are in direct conflict with our doctrine, social values and spiritual identity, and to rescue the youth by exposing and refuting these teachings and philosophies through biblical truth."[5] Leaders who are involved in the national youth ministry of the Hiwot Berhan Church share the same burden and passion for the youth in higher academic institutions.

The third cultural value I discovered during the interviews that is a threat to leadership development is the low estimation most cultures have for women. As a result, the annual intake of female students in the Bible schools is very low. Women comprise the majority in most local congregations. However, they are not invited to regional and national assemblies. The role of women in the leadership of the family and the church has not been given proper attention and recognition. The Hiwot Berhan Church leadership is obviously paternal. In churches such as Hiwot Berhan, neglecting the involvement of women in leadership is unnatural, non-Pentecostal, and unbiblical. It is unnatural because it is like avoiding half of the human race in their congregations. It is non-Pentecostal because world Pentecostals believe and practice that the outpouring of the Holy Spirit is for both men and women (Acts 2:17–21). And it is unbiblical because, first, it violates the doctrine of creation. God created male and female of the same essence and for the same purpose. Second, it violates the doctrine of salvation. Jesus died for the whole fallen human race, which includes the women of the world. Third, it violates the doctrine of the church. The church of God is composed of both men and women (Gal 3:28). Fourth, it violates the doctrine of New Testament ministry. New Testament ministry is one of grace sovereignly distributed by the Holy Spirit (1 Cor 12:11). It is gift-based ministry rather than gender-based ministry. If the sovereign God is the one who calls individuals to diverse ministries in the church, then church leaders may not impose their decision as to whom or which gender God should choose for his purpose.

Prior to my research, I observed several biblical principles of Christian leadership as essential for Hiwot Berhan leaders, pastoral leadership, and ministerial ethics. The most outstanding value in the minds of the participants was the spiritual formation of the leaders. Therefore I needed to address the leaders to be grounded in discipleship principles, to set an example to the congregation, and to establish a godly relationship with family and with the community at large. The second Christian and biblical value leaders need

---

5. Berhe, "Vision and Objective," 11.

is nurturing and managing one's family in a biblical manner. Elevating the status of women, children, and the youth in the family, church, and community by equipping them for leadership roles now is an urgent need for the multiplication of leaders in the church. The principles of servant leadership are highly recommended by participants in order to overcome some of the harmful cultural and secular leadership practices that have penetrated the church. Sound biblical and evangelical doctrines are timeless values that are currently desired by the leadership of the Hiwot Berhan churches. These doctrines include the Pentecostal and charismatic value of gift-based leadership and the Spirit-filled ministry of proclaiming the whole gospel for the whole person. False teachings and practices of a local and global nature are prevalent in both rural and urban areas. These false teachings and practices are related to physical health, material wealth, and earthly success. Therefore, holding to sound biblical teachings and practices is a timely value recommended by participants.

One of the major challenges for alternative leadership training in the context of the Hiwot Berhan Church is financial sustainability and the ability of the program to be self-supporting. The participants expressed their concern about the long-standing problem of the church's dependency on outside support for its training programs. Before requesting the financial partnership of the churches with the alternative leadership training program, the foundational work of mobilizing the churches through teaching the practice of Christian stewardship needs to be conducted. The existing formal theological institutions for resident trainees demand partnership and support from outside because libraries, computer laboratories, equipment, and facilities require large sums in funding. The Swedish Pentecostal Church and the Pentecostal Assemblies of Canada are already partnering with the church to support the resident theological colleges.

One other biblical value to be considered in developing church leaders is sharpening the preaching and teaching skills of the leaders. I observed that most of the regions the participants came from have potential trainers who know the language and culture of the trainees. Training these trainers by equipping them with teaching and communication skills can result in the transformation of local church leaders.

The Hiwot Berhan Church is large in population, geographical distribution, and cultural diversification, and needs to address, as a denomination, its leadership training need through one ideal institution or program. After the interviews, I observed that in order to address the leadership needs of such a denomination, the delivery system that would be efficient for the alternative leadership training would focus on selecting and equipping a few faithful trainers from each region so that they can go back and train the leaders of local churches in their areas. This training strategy will ensure the multiplication of emerging leaders needed now and in the future.

The literature supports the findings of this part of the research in many ways. The democratic values of election, the secular values of management, and the cultural values of having chieftains are discussed in the literature as threats to leadership development regionally as well as globally.[6] The cultural value of having a low estimation of women is shared by communities in Ethiopia, the rest of Africa, and Latin America, as discussed in the literature. However, Pentecostal and charismatic evangelicalism in Latin America has helped the churches overcome this threat by elevating the status of women at home, in the church, and in the community. The Hiwot Berhan Church is Pentecostal by confession and yet is not able to elevate the status of women in these areas. This practice of the church is paradoxical. The tension between the clergy and laity is also an unscriptural dichotomy that the Hiwot Berhan Church needs to overcome in order to promote the leadership development process. The Hiwot Berhan Church could imitate the example of Latin American Pentecostal and charismatic churches. The threat of ethnocentrism during the appointment of church leaders is one that the church in Ethiopia shares with many other churches on the continent of Africa. The line between a healthy ethnic affiliation and ethnocentrism is thin. Ethnocentrism gives birth to denominationalism, and denominationalism, in turn, gives multiple birth to contention, strife, division, and spiritual and missional stagnancy in the church.

The literature supports the findings on the recommended biblical and Christian values that enhance leadership development in the following ways. First, the literature supports the dissatisfaction that national church leaders both in Ethiopia and in other Majority World nations have with theological values that promote religious elitism. Second, the quest among national church leaders for biblical and Christian values that are relevant to their

---

6. Elliston, *Home Grown Leaders*, 11.

respective cultures is expressed in both the literature and the findings. Third, the literature and the research findings explicitly demonstrate that the cry of national church leaders in Ethiopia and many other Majority World nations is for leadership training to give priority to the spiritual formation of the trainees. Fourth, the findings and the literature also agree that leadership training needs to equip the trainees with skills such as preaching, writing, and administration. Fifth, equipping the intellect with knowledge should not be an end in itself. It is a means to an end, which is demonstrating Christlikeness in behavior and practicing skillfulness in preaching and leadership (Ps 78:72).

In the theological framework of Jesus's model of training the Twelve, Jesus warned the disciples that the secular values of lordship and the religious values of the Pharisees both promoted leadership as a status. The secular and religious leadership values of those times were threats to the leadership values in the community of the kingdom of God (Matt 20:10–28; 23:1–12). Jesus lived, taught, and transferred servanthood (Phil 2:5–11). Christian leadership is a call to pastoral leadership in which the shepherd feeds the flock and not himself or herself (Ezek 34; Phil 2:19–22; John 21:15–17; 1 Pet 5:1–4).

The findings in this portion of the research inform the ministry of the Hiwot Berhan Church to introduce two types of changes. First, the leaders of the church and the formal theological institutions are advised to conduct research among the people groups with whom they are working in order to identify the specific social and cultural values that are threats to leadership development. Second, the leaders of all the training programs of this church are recommended to design the curricula to be grounded on biblical and evangelical values to equip leaders so that they can overcome the threats from the social and cultural values dominant in their respective regions. I hope the leaders of the Hiwot Berhan Church and the officers of the formal theological institutions will critically investigate the relevancy of curricula before adopting them.

Ways of Making the Leadership Training Program Relevant, Sustainable, and Self-Supporting

My observations prior to the research concerning how to make leadership training relevant and financially sustainable were the use of vernaculars as a medium of instruction and raising funds domestically to support alternative leadership training. Through the research, I discovered three encouraging areas in which the churches can financially and materially partner with the leadership training programs. These are providing potential trainers, the availability of training venues and facilities, and the capacity individual trainees have to sponsor themselves and to purchase training materials.

However, the challenges the training faces outweigh the potential it has for relevancy and sustainability. First, the choice of media of instruction is complex because of the transition in the national educational policy since 1991. Second, the current status of the availability (or lack of availability) of the whole Bible in the vernaculars of the language groups I interviewed has implications for the relevancy of the training because contextualization becomes a reality if and when a people group have the Scriptures in their mother tongue. Third, the low literacy rate in most rural areas of Ethiopia is a clear hindrance to conducting training through literature. The two major challenges I observed as strongholds that need to be leveled to the ground for a smooth performance of alternative leadership training are the lack of training materials in the vernaculars and the sluggishness of the Hiwot Berhan churches in the knowledge and practice of Christian stewardship due to their long tradition of dependency on outside support for training. The Hiwot Berhan churches and the populations of believers in Jimma, Tigray, Amhara, and Dire Dawa are few, so financial support from outside is inevitable in order to assist the financially struggling congregations in these regions. One major finding from the focus group and individual interviews is that a nationwide mobilization of the local churches that are working under the Hiwot Berhan denomination through biblical teaching on Christian stewardship will create a preparedness of their hearts so that they are all spiritually motivated for the mission of the alternative leadership training program.

Two findings that are not supported by the literature in this research are the role of the literacy rate in sustaining leadership training and the availability of the Scriptures in the vernaculars in order to maintain the relevancy of a leadership training program. The other findings, such as the challenge of financial dependency on outside support, the foreignness of the media of instruction, and the lack of training materials written by native writers, are strongly supported by the literature in the research. The literature indicates that churches and theological institutions in Ethiopia, the rest of Africa, Asia, and Latin America share the same struggle in resolving the problems of the lack of teaching materials in the vernaculars, the use of the mother tongue as a medium of instruction, and the ability of leadership training programs to be financially self-supporting.

The biblical theological framework in this research implies that the following factors contributed to the success of Jesus's model of training the Twelve. First, the medium of instruction Jesus used was the language of the trainees. Second, Jesus's method of multiplication of leaders was to select a few disciples and equip them so that they, in turn, could equip others who would later rise to leadership. Third, Jesus depended on domestic material and financial resources to support himself and his disciples. The generosity of his close followers was the source of his income. The Christian tradition does not have evidence of Jesus writing training materials or any other kind of literature. However, his use of the Torah (Old Testament) gives a timeless example that trainers and trainees of all ages equally need to learn that the Scriptures are the primary and authoritative textbook for all Christian leadership training programs. In addition, Jesus himself is the living book, as the "But I tell you" statements of Matthew 5 imply. Although Jesus himself did not write a book, he later inspired his followers through his Spirit so that they were able to write about him and about what he had orally communicated to them when he was with them during the days of his life on earth. Biblical training is authoritative whereas academic training is opinion oriented. Biblical training says, "The Bible says . . .," whereas academic training says, "I think . . ." Biblical training has the apostolic teaching and faith as its content, spiritual empowerment as its goal, and reliability and giftedness as its entrance requirement (2 Tim 2:2).

Of all the findings of this research, the findings on the relevancy and sustainability of the leadership training program are the most challenging to the leadership of the Hiwot Berhan Church and the Bible schools it owns and operates. The leadership of the church is advised to make the following commitments. First, they need to accept the realities of the situation in the churches as revealed through this research. Second, they are recommended to conduct a broader research that includes participants from all churches working among diverse cultural groups so that they are able to assess the need in a comprehensive manner. Third, I highly recommend that the leaders of the Hiwot Berhan Church conduct a national campaign by mobilizing the churches for Christian stewardship through biblical teaching. Fourth, the church is also advised to select, organize, and motivate national writers so that they can produce relevant training materials in the vernaculars, which can then be used in the leadership training programs. Fifth, the leadership of the church needs to start selecting strategic training centers throughout the country, training venues that are accessible to trainees in specific regions. All in all, the findings in this category of research recommend the leadership of the church to design immediate and long-term plans that will enable the church to own and operate a relevant and financially sustainable leadership training program for the vocational and bivocational leaders who are laboring hard to meet the spiritual and moral needs of their respective congregations.

Implications of the Findings

This research is an outcome of my preplanned and preconceived ambition for church leadership training programs in Ethiopia. The findings of this research will help in two areas. First, they provide direction for the immediate future plan I envision to engage in developing church leaders in Ethiopia. I have already realized the following specific elements of direction: the need for an alternative training program for church leaders, the types of church leaders that need developing, the kinds of courses that need to be designed and produced, the types of delivery systems to consider, and the kinds of resources available domestically. Second, this research will be translated into Amharic with some modifications so that it can serve as a working document for the church leadership training project I am planning to implement in the immediate future here in Ethiopia among the evangelical churches.

This research will serve as my working document for the church leadership training institute that I have anticipated for over ten years. The leadership training program I want to implement in the near future will have the following design:

1. Mission: developing succeeding and successful leaders for the evangelical churches in Ethiopia;
2. Strategy: working in partnership with the evangelical churches, theological schools, and Christian organizations in Ethiopia to deliver the alternative leadership training program to church leaders;

3. Delivery system: conducting leadership training sessions, providing training materials in the vernaculars, mentoring potential and emerging church leaders;
4. Structure: board of governors, director of institute, regional coordinators, and trainers;
5. Venues: national office and coordinating center in Addis Ababa, regional training and coordinating centers at Hawassa (south), Bahir Dar (north), Jimma (west), Dire Dawa (east), and church facilities and theological schools;
6. Financial resources: training fees from trainees, training material sales, special offerings from churches through fundraising programs, and special donations from generous individuals and organizations within the country;
7. Trainees: leaders of local churches who have the basic skills of reading and writing and who are also serving either as vocational and bivocational leaders;
8. Cycles: one cycle will have the duration of one month with four cycles in a year; one course will be given for five days;
9. Trainers: I will establish a network among the alumni of the theological institutes where I have been teaching and leading for the last twenty-two years (see tables 5.2 and 5.3).

The findings of this research have implications for the content and delivery systems of the training programs that are owned and operated by the Hiwot Berhan Church of Ethiopia:

- This research was conducted among limited cultures in which the Hiwot Berhan Church operates. The church is expected to conduct a broader assessment of the training needs among its congregations that are located among the rest of Ethiopia's diverse cultures.
- The findings indicate that a program and curriculum review is needed for the formal theological institutions to make their content relevant and their delivery systems context oriented.
- The formal theological institutions are few in number. Their annual intake is insignificant compared with the size of the congregations and the training need expressed. In addition,

Table 5.2 Basic Leadership Training

Cycles	Courses	Days
First cycle: Bible division		
	Introduction to the Bible	5 days
	Devotional reading of the Bible	5 days
	1 Corinthians	5 days
	Psalms for worship	5 days
Second cycle: theology division		
	Survey of Christian doctrines	5 days
	The nature of heresies and how to refute them	5 days
	The work of the Holy Spirit	5 days
	Biblical demonology and deliverance	5 days
Third cycle: ministry division		
	The ministry of the Word	5 days
	Church administration	5 days
	Discipleship	5 days
	Evangelism and church planting	5 days
Fourth cycle: holistic division		
	Spiritual formation part 1	5 days
	The theology of work	5 days
	Christian stewardship	5 days
	Marriage and family	5 days

three of the Bible schools are located in the southern part of the country. They are not easily accessible to the churches in the north, west, and east of the country. Therefore, the leadership of the Hiwot Berhan Church of Ethiopia needs to plan how to make leadership training accessible to areas that are at a distance from the existing Bible schools.

- The church is still facing dependency syndrome because of its long-standing partnership with mission organizations from abroad. The leadership of the church should teach Christian stewardship in order to raise money domestically to make the leadership training programs self-supporting and sustainable.

Table 5.3 Advanced Leadership Training

Cycles	Courses	Days
First cycle: Bible division		
	Study of Bible books part 1	5 days
	Study of Bible books part 2	5 days
	Controversies, councils, and creeds	5 days
	Interpretation and study methods of Scripture	5 days
Second cycle: theology division		
	God and angels	5 days
	Humanity and sin	5 days
	Salvation	5 days
	The church and the end times	5 days
Third cycle: ministry division		
	The theology of ministry	5 days
	The gifts of the Holy Spirit	5 days
	Christian leadership	5 days
	The mission of God	5 days
Fourth cycle: holistic division		
	Media and ministry	5 days
	Principles of teaching and training	5 days
	Mentoring for leadership	5 days
	Spiritual formation part 2	5 days

- The existing formal theological institutions do not have standard textbooks and relevant training materials. The findings of this research indicate the need for relevant teaching materials that meet the needs of the trainees. The leadership of the theological institutions of the Hiwot Berhan Church have a lot of assignments waiting for them in the area of producing relevant textbooks for the Bible schools.
- The findings also showed the lack of spiritually and academically qualified trainers for both the existing theological institutions and the alternative training programs recommended in this research. The leaders of the church are advised to start recruiting and

developing trainers who will be qualified to equip the thousands of vocational and bivocational leaders who are currently serving among the vast rural areas of the nation.
- The Hiwot Berhan Church leadership may also consider the formation of a domestic accreditation department (or an internal curriculum endorsement section) that will maintain the academic standards of its theological institutions and training programs.

The findings of this research will also have implications for other evangelical churches in Ethiopia. These churches minister in similar social and cultural environments to the Hiwot Berhan Church. They share the cultural values, economic factors, academic limitations, and potential ministry opportunities of the nation. The implications of this research for these other evangelical churches in Ethiopia are as follows:

- The evangelical churches need to ensure that the training programs for church leaders are research based, meaning that an assessment of training needs is conducted before introducing or adopting leadership training programs.
- The theological institutions that are owned and operated by the evangelical churches in Ethiopia need to consider making program and curriculum reviews in order to deliver relevant theological education to the leadership of the churches.
- Evangelical churches in Ethiopia should develop and produce relevant training materials in the vernaculars of trainees. The churches may also need to consider reviewing the media of instruction in their training programs, especially those conducted for church leaders in rural areas.
- The process of contextualization of leadership training programs is possible only when diverse ethnic groups in the nation have the Scriptures in their vernaculars. Therefore, the evangelical churches in Ethiopia are advised to speed up the translation and availability of the Scriptures primarily in the major languages of the peoples in the country.
- Lack of faithful stewardship of God's resources is one area this research has discovered. Dependency on outside subsidies is a challenge common to most evangelical churches in Ethiopia.

- Therefore, the leadership of evangelical churches are advised through the findings of this research to teach their congregations Christian stewardship and to practice raising money domestically in order to ensure the sustainability of church leadership training programs.
- Trainers who are required for theological institutions and for church-based leadership training are expected to have basic qualifications. They need to acquire academic degrees; they need to demonstrate the gift and skill of teaching; they need to model godly character; and they must have a proven ministry experience in the local church. This research indicates the lack of a sufficient number of qualified trainers in the theological institutions and churches. The evangelical churches and the theological institutions in Ethiopia need to work hand in hand to multiply trainers who are qualified spiritually, academically, morally, and experientially.

The findings of this research also have specific implications for the formal theological institutions operating at an undergraduate level. These institutions can learn the following lessons:

- They can learn the basic lesson that their programs must be research based in identifying the needs and purposes of the learners and the churches for which they are providing a service.
- They need to identify through research who the ideal graduate is and what types of ideal leaders their respective institutions are supposed to produce.
- They need to build a strong relationship with their denomination and/or their constituencies so that they are able to serve the purpose of the churches in the nation.
- They must be willing to review their curricula in order to receive renewed interest from learners and churches by providing courses that are relevant and marketable.
- They need to review their delivery systems by taking the livelihoods and interests of learners in both rural and urban settings into consideration.

- They need to consider the availability of textbooks in the vernaculars, the accessibility of their training programs to the majority of learners, the relevancy of the medium of instruction, and the financial sustainability of the training programs.

The findings of this research will have global implications in reminding churches and formal theological institutions that are struggling with Western models of education to consider revising their mission, objectives, curricula, organizational structure, and entire programs. Evangelical churches and theological institutions serving in Africa, Asia, and Latin America share some of the challenges that Ethiopia is facing in the area of developing ideal church leaders for the twenty-first century. The formal theological institutions in these parts of the world need to review their mission, curricula, delivery systems, media of instruction, training materials, types of trainees, organizational structure, and leadership regularly and rigorously on the basis of scientific research. The findings of this research are warnings of how the Western model of training has caused a divorce between church and theological training, and churches and theological institutions in Africa, Asia, and Latin America need to work toward training models that can reunite the church and its leadership training program.

Limitations of the Study

This qualitative research was conducted within the context of a single evangelical denomination, the Hiwot Berhan Church of Ethiopia. I formed only four focus groups, the participants of which came from just a few specifically selected regions in Ethiopia. The total number of participants in the focus group interviews and in one-on-one interviews was thirty. The purpose of the interviews was to explore the need of the church in one area: the need for an alternative church leadership model. Therefore, the research has limitations in the areas of research topic, number of participants, and coverage of research field:

- This research was done within a single evangelical denomination. The findings from the Hiwot Berhan Church may not fully represent the leadership training needs of other evangelical churches in Ethiopia and elsewhere in every respect.

- The findings from this research may not represent the leadership training needs in other churches, such as the Ethiopian Orthodox Tewahedo Church and the Ethiopian Catholic Church, as these churches are accomplishing tremendous work in educational fields in contexts different from those of the Hiwot Berhan Church of Ethiopia.
- The findings of this research may not apply fully to evangelical and Pentecostal churches in Ethiopia that have indigenous roots and that have been financially self-supporting from the time of their establishment.
- The mission, curricula, and organization of the formal theological institutions of the Hiwot Berhan Church might be different from those of the theological institutions that are run by other evangelical denominations. Therefore, the findings of this research about the formal theological institutions may have limitations in representing the facts in other theological institutions in the country.
- The findings about the theological institutions in this research are based on undergraduate programs; they may not fully apply to theological institutions at the graduate level.
- The research was conducted in the context of eight ethnic groups. With the Oromo and the Amhara being the two largest populations, these eight ethnic groups represent the broader population of the country. However, the research does not include participants from some of the other major ethnic groups, such as Gambela, Benishangul, Ethiopian Somali, and Afar.
- Women and young people are the largest part of the population in Ethiopia. These two groups are not represented among the participants in a proportional number.
- Most of the participants had never before experienced a group interview in a research context. Some of them, especially those from southwestern Ethiopia, confused research with expression of grievances and an official appeal to denominational leadership. The process of selection of the participants had limitations because the participants came from vast geographical areas. The participants knew me for my critical thinking in my approach to

matters related to ministry. I also have a sense of humor. These factors helped greatly in creating openness and confidentiality in the interviews. However, one of the research team members was a key denominational leader, which helped me even more because the participants spoke openly and critically in order to be heard by him.

- The findings of this research came from participants who lived and served mostly in rural settings because most of the local congregations of the Hiwot Berhan Church are located in rural Ethiopia. The leadership training needs for urban churches might not be adequately addressed in this research.

- The social and cultural values recorded in this research are the expressions of the participants. They are not verified by other written sources or by further research on the culture of the ethnic groups of the participants.

Unexpected Observations

I have been excited and also humbled by some of the facts that I discovered during the process of this research. First, the agreement between the leaders of the church in the Gofa area and the state administration of the Gamo Gofa zone on the role of church leaders in political involvement greatly surprised me. Those who took the initiative to establish guidance for the relationship between the church and state were state administrators and not church leaders. Second, the Hiwot Berhan Church working among the Nyangatom people is a financially struggling church that is still subsidized from the national office, and yet to hear them sharing that they had crossed the geographical border to South Sudan and had won two hundred new converts who were waiting for water baptism was for me both a surprise and a paradox.

Third, the evangelical churches working in the North Shewa zone had contextualized their ministry so much that they observed the religious holidays of the Ethiopian Orthodox Tewahedo Church by abstaining from manual agricultural tasks and by dedicating those days for training and revival meetings. Fourth, what I discovered about the necessity of the availability of the Scriptures in the vernaculars of trainees was a surprise. The relevancy of the training depended on the availability of Bible translations in the languages of the trainees. Fifth, the low literacy rate among the rural communities of Ethiopia was a surprise to me in revealing another challenge for the sustainability of the alternative leadership training program in rural churches. Sixth, the distinction the participants of the focus groups made in the use of the terms "leader" and "minister" surprised me. It was not that I did not know the existence of a distinction between vocational and bivocational leaders within the evangelical churches here in Ethiopia. What shocked me was that the participants assumed that the "leaders" were bivocational while "ministers" were the vocational workers who were not assumed to be "leaders."

Seventh, the greatest surprise I had was when I heard from the Sidama focus group that the primary qualification anticipated of the ideal church leader was that the candidate was wealthy enough to provide for the needs of his or her family, because, first, the leader has to prove that he or she can manage his or her family well; second, he or she has to be hospitable by welcoming guest preachers to stay in his or her home; and third, he or she is advised to be generous enough to sponsor some of the church ministries and projects. The leader in this context is the bivocational leader elected to the leadership role in the local church. I have lived and served among the Hiwot Berhan churches in the Sidama area for nearly forty-two years. I have facilitated the appointment of leaders in the local churches on several occasions during those years. I have hammered home the spiritual and moral qualifications found in 1 Timothy 3 and Titus 1. However, I did not discover this community value that was in the minds of dear Sidama believers when I conducted leadership appointment sessions among them on different occasions.

Recommendations

The findings of this research can introduce changes in the practice of leadership training in the following ways. First, churches that are engaged in leadership training are recommended to identify the types of ideal church leaders that are expected by the churches in their specific region. Second, churches and formal theological institutions need to jointly make an assessment of the social and cultural values that create threats to leadership development in their specific culture. Third, churches and theological schools should explore the biblical and Christian values that are recommended by the churches that are sending their trainees to the leadership training programs. Fourth, every church and theological school that is planning to pioneer a leadership training program is advised to ensure the cultural relevancy and financial sustainability of the program from its beginning.

Based on the limitations of the scope of this research, I recommend that extensive and comprehensive research be conducted in the following areas:

1. The social and cultural values that shape the thought patterns of church leaders and congregants in different cultures in Ethiopia should be researched as a valuable resource for churches and theological institutions.
2. The contributions and limitations of formal theological institutions that are operated by the evangelical denominations in Ethiopia need additional extensive research in order to bridge the structural gap between the institutions and the churches.
3. The Ethiopian Orthodox Tewahedo Church and the religion of Islam have the largest numbers of adherents in the nation. These two religions have shaped the worldview of the majority of the Ethiopian population. The impact these two major religious groups have on the leadership values of the evangelical churches requires separate research.
4. The dichotomy, tension, and harmony between vocational and bivocational leaders in the history of the evangelical churches in Ethiopia are phenomenal research fields that will contribute to leadership development programs in the country.
5. This research focused on a few selected cultural church groups. A wider representation in the focus groups of the diverse cultural groups that exist in Ethiopia would be necessary to produce a comprehensive finding that will represent the church leadership training needs nationwide. This kind of extensive research topic requires a separate study.
6. Through the interviews with the participants, I discovered that initial research into the general leadership problems in evangelical churches of Ethiopia would have been beneficial to lay the foundations for further research on church leadership.
7. Independent research on the leadership training needs for evangelical churches working in urban areas is also a vast area of exploration that will benefit both churches and theological institutions.

Postscript

I traveled about 2,200 kilometers to the four interview sites – Bahir Dar (Amhara region), Adola (Guji zone), Hawassa (Sidama zone), and Wolayita Sodo (southwest Ethiopia). I conducted five leadership seminars on the Eight Core Values of Christian Leadership designed by the International Leadership Institute (ILI), and that gave me access to 447 leaders. The written and oral feedback I received from the trainees, my own observations from my physical presence at research sites, and the formal research I conducted helped me to gather firsthand information on the need for leadership training for church leaders.

First, I discovered that leadership was the most widely discussed and debated topic among the leaders of the Hiwot Berhan Church and even other evangelical churches. Second, the request from the informal training participants for the continuity of such training was a clear indication of the need for a paradigm shift in leadership training among them. Third, I was encouraged to see the rise of a younger generation of potential leaders in the Hiwot Berhan churches at the local, regional, and national levels. These are the candidates who will be eligible for the alternative leadership training programs conducted in the near future. Fourth, my discovery of the financial capability and stewardship of the Hiwot Berhan Church leaders, especially those from rural churches, to purchase Christian books each worth about 100 Ethiopian birr was promising for the sustainability of the alternative church leadership training program I plan to conduct. Fifth, I sensed a wave of national awareness among the Hiwot Berhan Church leaders for a change in and reform of the qualifications, selection process, style, duties, and accountability of church leaders in order for the church to be able to fulfill its mission to believers as well as to the wider community. Sixth, the sustainability of the alternative leadership training program depends on the availability of writers and trainers who can conduct the training in the vernacular. In my tour around the churches I discovered that the number of leaders with graduate and postgraduate degrees in biblical theology within the Hiwot Berhan churches was less than twenty. In light of the size of the denomination (about three thousand congregations and an estimated population of three million), the number of academically qualified ministers is like a drop in the ocean. The Hiwot Berhan Church should develop trainers, writers, and researchers who are academically qualified with formal training at a graduate and postgraduate level.

In this research I discovered the elements that are essential for alternative church leadership training in the context of the Hiwot Berhan Church. These elements include identifying the ideal church leader, evaluating how effective the existing formal theological institutions are in producing the ideal church leader, discovering values that are hindrances to and values that help leadership development, establishing the type of alternative leadership training that can produce the ideal church leader, and exploring ways to make the training relevant and financially sustainable. However, it is important to remind readers that even well-organized and well-facilitated training programs are not ends in themselves. Biblical training is a means to an end. It is purposeful. My text for the theological framework of this research was Mark 3:13–19. Walter W. Wessel makes the following comment on this passage: "The training was not an end in itself – [the disciples] were to be sent out to preach the Good News and to drive out demons."[7] The training of the Twelve culminates with them being commissioned for the task for which they were trained (Mark 6:6–13). Jesus's training was not an end in itself. It was a purposeful training. Jesus had his God-given objectives as his mission here on earth. In the training program that Jesus conducted, the type of training, the purpose of the training, and the place of ministry appointment were interrelated and integrated. Wessel comments from Mark 6:12–13 on the purpose for which Jesus trained the disciples:

> Mark now describes the actual mission of the Twelve. It was clearly patterned after Jesus' own ministry: (1) preaching repentance, (2) driving out demons, and (3) healing the sick. By these activities they were demonstrating that the kingdom of God had come with power. At this point, their mission is a mere extension of the ministry of Jesus.[8]

Jesus appointed and trained the twelve apostles so that they would continue the task he had already begun. They continued the ministry with the power

---

7. Wessel, "Mark," 150.
8. Wessel, 159.

and authority he delegated to them. His training was a means to this purposeful end.

The alternative church leadership training that is recommended for the Hiwot Berhan Church in this research is not an end in itself, either. The training elements explored in this research include purpose and objectives in the training package. The purpose and objectives of the alternative leadership training program for the Hiwot Berhan Church are grounded in the concerns expressed by the participants, the observations of the researcher, and the recommendations of the 447 leaders who attended the training on the Eight Core Values of Effective Christian Leadership designed by ILI. The purpose and objectives of the alternative church leadership training program for the Hiwot Berhan Church include the following items:

1. Biblical discipleship with the goal of nurturing and maturing both the leadership and the congregants;
2. Empowerment with passion for cross-cultural evangelism and church planting with the goal of bringing unreached nations to Christ through the proclamation of the gospel;
3. Multiplication of leaders with a pastoral gift who can demonstrate the skills of preaching, teaching, and leading with the goal of equipping and mobilizing the churches for Christian stewardship; and
4. Equipping trainers who have the gift of teaching with the long-term goal of maintaining the sustainability of the alternative leadership training program.

In order to accomplish these objectives, the leadership of the alternative leadership training program in the Hiwot Berhan Church needs to consider several biblical principles. First, the entrance requirement for enrollment in the alternative leadership training program should primarily focus on those candidates who demonstrate the gift and potential of Christian leadership. The Bible says, "Instruct the wise and they will be wiser still; teach the righteous and they will add to their learning" (Prov 9:9). During the construction of the tabernacle God instructed Moses, saying, "Also I have given ability to all the skilled workers to make everything I have commanded you" (Exod 31:6b). The New Testament ministry is a gift-based ministry. A leadership development program has to ensure that trainees are those who have already demonstrated leadership skills in their respective local churches. The Hiwot Berhan Church leaders are advised to invest their God-given resources in trainees who have shown evidence of a leadership capacity in the ministry areas to which they have been assigned.

Second, not everyone with a title of leadership may qualify for leadership training. Every leader and congregant needs training in discipleship and the general ministry of the church. However, leadership training is meant for the few faithful stewards who have proven themselves as equippers. The Bible says, "And the things you have heard me say in the presence of many witnesses entrust to reliable people who will also be qualified to teach others" (2 Tim 2:2). The alternative leadership training program should not recruit nominal leaders simply to do justice to all. The leaders of the alternative leadership training program in the Hiwot Berhan Church need to consider these two biblical qualifications for trainees: the moral qualification of reliability and the qualification of the skill of teaching. These factors will ensure the sustainability of the training program and also prove good stewardship of God-given resources, such as the proper management of human, material, and financial resources.

In 2015 the Hiwot Berhan Church of Ethiopia celebrated the fiftieth anniversary of the outpouring of the Holy Spirit. It happened in Hawassa in August 1965. The Swedish Pentecostal Mission was holding its annual training at Hawassa. Ethiopian church leaders and young students from the university and from teacher training institutes were attending the three-week training. Pastor Joseph Mattson Bose from the USA and pastor Omaha Cha-cha from Kenya were the guest speakers. According to eyewitnesses, the participants from all over the nation were fasting and praying on one of the Wednesdays. That evening, God poured out his Spirit upon the participants. Nearly everyone in the church building was baptized in the Holy Spirit, demonstrated by their speaking in tongues. Although there were individuals and groups who experienced the baptism of the Holy Spirit and speaking in tongues prior to this event, that occasion in Hawassa in August 1965 was recorded and is remembered as the Pentecost of the Hiwot Berhan Church.

I had the privilege of visiting a historical site in Guji land in May 2014 as I was traveling to gather my data for this research. The place is called Denbobi and is located about four hundred kilometers south of Addis Ababa. Seven young people from the Guji-Oromo ethnic group came to acknowledge Jesus

Christ as their Savior and Lord in 1978. Their Christian confession resulted in persecution and abandonment by their parents and the community. They spent weeks in the nearby forest hiding and praying. God in his sovereign power visited them by pouring out his Spirit on the seven in 1979. They were all baptized in the Holy Spirit and spoke in tongues as evidence of that baptism. In May 2014 I met five of them – Pastor Elias Kebede and four others from the group. The Hiwot Berhan Church in Guji-Oromo area commemorates the year 1979 as its year of Pentecost.

In connection with this, one of the biblical values that the participants recommended to be considered in the alternative leadership training program was a restoration of the Pentecostal experience and distinctive. I recommend to the leadership of the Hiwot Berhan Church the following ways to restore and maintain the distinctive of Pentecostal teaching and practice:

1. Teach the leadership and the congregations about the person and work of the Holy Spirit. The work of the Holy Spirit in regeneration, sanctification, and empowerment for ministry needs to be taught and understood distinctly;
2. Encourage each believer in the Hiwot Berhan Church, both young and senior, to experience the baptism of the Holy Spirit personally through prayer, by the laying on of hands, and by continuously seeking the infilling of the Holy Spirit (Acts 2:1–4; 19:1–7; Eph 5:18–20);
3. Restore the tradition of holding annual conventions with an emphasis on the charismatic work of the Holy Spirit and on prayer for nationwide revival as used to be the case in the 1960s;
4. Instruct believers to identify the spiritual gifts, to seek them earnestly, and to practice them by faith and in an orderly manner (Rom 12:3–8; 1 Cor 12–14; Eph 4:11);
5. Equip the leadership with scriptural knowledge so that they are able to discern and evaluate the soundness of the content and delivery of the manifestations of the spiritual gifts;
6. Review and reform the curricula of the formal theological institutions so that they give adequate emphasis to the Pentecostal distinctive through the courses they are offering;

7. Pentecostals believe that the New Testament ministry is gift-based. This conviction leads to the understanding that Christian leadership is a God-given ability that individuals receive through spiritual empowerment. Therefore, the Hiwot Berhan leaders need to hold to this biblical and Pentecostal value in order to overcome some of the secular values such as leadership appointment by vote, which has become a cause of chaos in the church during times of leadership selection; and
8. Develop a Pentecostal theology and a Pentecostal biblical interpretation that is scripturally sound and contextually relevant in order to guide the charismatic movement in a missionally productive and morally decent pattern.

The findings of this research have enabled me to renew my personal ministry commitment. After the completion of my current study, my immediate plan is to design, direct, and discharge a church leadership training program that is relevant in content and accessible to the majority of leaders. I am also committed to start preparing training materials in the vernacular in three directions. First, I will write some of the training materials as I have already begun to do. Second, I am planning to organize writers with basic theological knowledge and with the skill and experience of writing Christian materials so that I can speed up the production of training materials in the vernacular. Third, I need to recruit people who are able to translate these training materials into some of the major languages in Ethiopia in order to meet the needs of church leaders who can only read and understand their mother tongue. My main strategy to implement the alternative leadership training programs will be to partner with evangelical denominations, formal theological institutions, Christian missions, and Christian organizations to conduct the training of trainers. Mentoring emerging leaders on a one-to-one basis and as a group will be my other commitment in order to identify those potential trainers for the continuity and sustainability of the alternative leadership training program. I envision the establishment of a national institute that serves as a center to train church leaders with the mission of developing succeeding and successful leaders for the churches in Ethiopia and in the Horn of Africa (Eritrea, Djibouti, Somalia, South Sudan, and Sudan).

In reality, most of what I observed during the research was a revalidation of what I had already felt about my church because I have been an active participant in the ministry of the Hiwot Berhan Church for over four decades. However, the observations I made this time were purposeful and done with a renewed and more seasoned mind as a result of my academic and spiritual exposure at the Beeson International Leadership Center. This research is my seedbed. The trees will grow up as I plant and water the seeds in the hearts and minds of leadership trainees on Ethiopian soil.

Appendix A

Summary of the Population of People Groups Represented by the Cultural Focus Groups of the Hiwot Berhan Church

People Group	Population
Guji	1,386,800
Jimma zone	2,486,155
Sidama	2,954,136
Gamo Gofa	1,593,104
Wolayita	1,501,112
Nyangatom	17,640
Jimma special zone	120,960
North Shewa zone (Oromia)	1,431,305
North Shewa zone (Amhara)	1,837,490
Dire Dawa	300,067

Source: Central Statistical Agency of Ethiopia, *Population and Housing Census 2007*.

Appendix B

Components of Expert Review

I selected a team of experts to evaluate the researcher-designed, semistructured interview questions prepared for the focus groups. The expert review had the following three components:

1. The names of the experts: three to four experts chosen from various academic backgrounds and experiences;
2. A letter of information sent to each expert, including the purpose of the research, the problem the research was addressing, the research questions, and the interview questions; and
3. A protocol form to be completed and returned to me to help the experts easily express their evaluation and feedback concerning the type and size of the interview questions.

Appendix C

Interview Protocol for Focus Groups

1. What are the training elements needed by the leaders in the Hiwot Berhan Church of Ethiopia at the local, regional, and national levels?
    1.1 What does an ideal church leader look like in your area?
    1.2 How effective are the existing formal theological institutions in producing that kind of church leader?
    1.3 What type of alternative training is needed to produce that kind of church leader?
    1.4 What delivery systems make the best sense to deliver the content?
    1.5 What other characteristics are unique to this region that we must consider when preparing local church leaders for this region?
2. How can these alternative leadership training elements be grounded in evangelical scriptural knowledge?
    2.1 What are the social and cultural leadership values that are threats to church leadership development?
    2.2 What biblical and Christian values does your group recommend to produce the types of church leaders you anticipate?

3. What is your recommendation about ways of making the leadership training program relevant, sustainable, and self-supporting?
   3.1 What is the medium of instruction that is relevant for the trainees in your area in order to make the alternative leadership training program effective?
   3.2 What types of national teachers and trainers who can conduct leadership training programs in the vernacular are available in your region?
   3.3 What kinds of leadership training materials are available in the vernacular in your region?
   3.4 What types of training venues and facilities that can accommodate trainees are available in your region?
   3.5 What types of vocational and bivocational trainees are available for the leadership training program in your region?
   3.6 How can the church in this region partner with leadership training programs in financial areas in order to make the training sustainable and self-supporting?

Appendix D

Interview Protocol for Individuals

1. What are the training elements needed by the leaders in the Hiwot Berhan Church of Ethiopia at the local, regional, and national level?
    1.1 What does an ideal church leader look like in your area?
    1.2 How effective are the existing formal theological institutions in producing that kind of church leader?
    1.3 What type of alternative training is needed to produce that kind of church leader?
    1.4 What delivery systems make the best sense to deliver the content?
    1.5 What other characteristics are unique to this region that we must consider when preparing local church leaders for this region?
2. How can these alternative leadership training elements be grounded in evangelical scriptural knowledge?
    2.1 What are the social and cultural leadership values that are threats to church leadership development?
    2.2 What biblical and Christian values does your group recommend to produce the types of church leaders you anticipate?

3. What is your recommendation about ways of making the leadership training program relevant, sustainable, and self-supporting?
   3.1 What is the medium of instruction that is preferred by the trainees in your area?
   3.2 What types of national teachers and trainers who can conduct leadership training programs in the vernacular are available in your region?
   3.3 What kinds of leadership training materials are available in the vernacular in your region?
   3.4 What types of training venues and facilities that can accommodate trainees are available in your region?
   3.5 What types of vocational and bivocational trainees are available for the leadership training program in your region?
   3.6 How can the church in this region partner with leadership training programs in financial areas in order to make the training sustainable and self-supporting?

Appendix E

Curriculum for Loke Bible School

No.	First Year/First Semester	First Year/Second Semester
1	Introductory English	Proper theology and bibliology
2	Introduction to computer	Foundation of missions
3	Communications	Historical and wisdom literature
4	Spirit-filled life	Synoptic Gospels and Acts
5	Hermeneutics	Introduction to Christian education
6	Pentateuch	Freshman English
	Second Year/First Semester	**Second Year/Second Semester**
1	Christology and soteriology	General epistles
2	Major and Minor Prophets	Pneumatology and angelology
3	NT2 – Pauline epistles	Addressing contemporary issues in society
4	Principles and methods of teaching	Principles of preaching
5	Understanding EOTC*	Understanding Islam
6	Introduction to leadership	Biblical ethics
7	Evangelism and church planting	The church and the last things

*EOTC is the Ethiopian Orthodox Tewahedo Church

Appendix F

Curriculum for Pentecostal Theological College

The Bachelor of Art in Christian Leadership is designed for those who are highly involved in church leadership and Christian organizations. The program provides a critical look at biblical leadership and its practical application in today's church. The program equips the students to deal with the changes and challenges of the church and its growth.

The Bachelor of Art in Christian Leadership program has 130 credit hours.

Divisions and required credit hours:
Compulsory courses 69 credit hours
Major courses 42 credit hours
Elective courses 15 credit hours
Major project 4 credit hours
Practicum
Total 130

Compulsory Courses

BIB	Division of Biblical Studies	21 Credit Hours
	Hermeneutics I	3
	Pentateuch	3
	Historical literature & wisdom literature	3
	Major Prophets & Minor Prophets	3
	Synoptic Gospels and Acts	3
	Pauline epistles	3
	General epistles/Johannine epistles, Hebrew, James, Jude, 1 & 2 Peter	3
THE	Division of Theological Studies	12 Credit Hours
	Proper theology & bibliology	3
	Christology & soteriology	3
	Pneumatology & angelology	3
	Ecclesiology & eschatology	3
CHM	Division of Church Ministries	12 Credit Hours
	Intro to Christian education	3
	Principles & methods of teaching	3
	Addressing contemporary issues in society	3
	Intro to counseling – biblical ethics	3
MIS	Division of Mission	3 Credit Hours
	Foundations of missions	3
GED	Division of General Studies	21 Credit hours
199	Introductory English	3
200	Freshman English	3
201	Sophomore English	3
	Critical thinking & logic	3
222	Intro to computer – exegesis for exposition	3
	Intro to psychology	3
	Research methodology	3

Specialization/Major Courses

LED	Division of Leadership Studies	42 Credit Hours
300	Intro to leadership	3
302	Spiritual foundations of leadership	3
313	Financial management	3
301	Leadership lessons from Nehemiah	3
304	Servant leadership	3
305	Conflict resolution	3
307	Leading in Christian education – leadership ministry	3
306	Team building	3
310	Intro to management	3
309	Church administration	3
315	Entrepreneurship and small business	3
317	Organizational behaviors	3
321	Human and material management	3
308	Ethics and leadership	3

Elective

CHM	Division of Church Ministries	15 Credit Hours
	Small group ministries – understanding Islam	3
	Understanding world religion – church history	3
	Christian home – understanding the Orthodox Church	3
THE	Division of Theological Studies	3
	Spiritual gifts – Spirit-filled life	3
	Distinctive of Pentecostal doctrine	3
	Apologetics	3
BIB	Division of Biblical Studies	3
	1 Corinthians	3

Major project 4 credit hours

Pentecostal Theological College Bachelor of Art in Christian Leadership Program Course Sequence[1]

Full-time students are supposed to take courses in the following sequence in order to finish the BTh program in four years:

Year 1, Semester 1

1. Introductory English
2. Intro to computer
3. Basic communication
4. Spirit-filled life
5. Hermeneutics
6. Pentateuch
7. Critical thinking & logic

Year 1, Semester 2

1. Freshman English
2. Proper theology & bibliology
3. Historical literature & wisdom literature
4. Synoptic Gospels and Acts
5. Intro to Christian education
6. Biblical ethics

Year 2, Semester 1

1. Christology & soteriology
2. Major Prophets & Minor Prophets
3. Pauline epistles
4. Principles & methods of teaching
5. Understanding EOTC
6. Foundations of missions

---

1. Source: Pentecostal Theological College, *Catalogue*.

Year 2, Semester 2

1. General epistles/Johannine epistles, Hebrew, James, Jude, 1 & 2 Peter
2. Pneumatology & angelology
3. Addressing contemporary issues in society
4. How to preach
5. Understanding Islam
6. Intro to leadership
7. Ecclesiology & eschatology

Year 3, Semester 1

1. Understanding world religion
2. Spiritual foundations of leadership
3. Sophomore English
4. Intro to management
5. Distinctive of Pentecostal doctrine
6. Research methodology

Year 3, Semester 2

1. Organizational behaviors
2. Servant leadership
3. Intro to psychology
4. Intro to counseling
5. Small-group ministries
6. Spiritual gifts
7. Financial management

Year 4, Semester 1

1. Team building
2. Entrepreneurship and small business
3. Human and material management
4. Apologetics
5. Distinctive of Pentecostal doctrine
6. Expository preaching
7. Christian home

Year 4, Semester 2
1. Ethics and leadership
2. Conflict resolution
3. Leading in Christian education
4. Church administration
5. Leadership lessons from Nehemiah
6. Major project

APPENDIX G

Curriculum for Adola Bible School

First Cycle	Second Cycle
Old Testament survey	Sport for evangelism
Doctrine	New Testament survey
Pastoral leadership	Methods of Bible study and interpretation
Administration of church property	Health
Conflict resolution	Preaching techniques
Prayer and worship	Christian marriage
The lists and operation of spiritual gifts	How to defend against heresies
Evangelism	The doctrine of Christ

APPENDIX H

Curriculum for Worancha Bible School

No.	First Cycle	Second Cycle
1	Old Testament survey	Survey of Christian doctrine
2	Harmful cultural practices	Evangelism and church planting
3	Christian ethics	Communication and conflict resolution
4	Management	Prayer and worship
5	Understanding Islam	Christian family and counseling
6	Understanding EOTC	Exegesis and hermeneutics
7	Church history	Church ordinances
8	The doctrine of God and the Bible	New Testament survey
	Third Cycle	**Fourth Cycle**
1	Homiletics	Heresies and apologetics
2	Spiritual gifts and the fruit of the Spirit	The doctrine of Christ and salvation
3	The four gospels	Christian marriage
4	1 and 2 Corinthians	The doctrine of angels
5	Entrepreneurship	Principles and methods of teaching
6	The church and its mission	Discipleship
7	The doctrine of humanity and sin	The doctrine of the church and end times
8	Church education and children's ministry	The theology of ministry

APPENDIX I

Ways in Which Churches Can Partner to Make Leadership Training Programs Culturally Relevant and Financially Sustainable

Participants	Medium of Instruction	Types of National Trainers Available	Types of Training Facilities Available
HBC focus group from the Amhara region	Primarily Amharic, diverse ethnic languages in the rural churches	Potentially available	A kindergarten and elementary school building, local church facilities
HBC focus group from the Guji-Oromo area	Primarily Oromigna, English as second option for the new generation of leaders	Potentially available	A Bible school facility, local church buildings
HBC focus group from the Sidama zone	Primarily Sidamigna in class supported by training materials in Amharic	Potentially available	Two Bible school facilities, local church buildings
HBC focus group from southwest Ethiopia	Primarily Amharic, diverse ethnic languages in rural settings	Potentially available	A kindergarten and elementary school facility, local church buildings, a training center, a rental guesthouse
HBC leader from the Tigray region	Tigrigna	Very few available with formal theological training	Local church buildings in urban centers, a rental guesthouse
HBC leader from the Jimma zone	Primarily Oromigna, diverse ethnic languages in rural areas, Amharic in urban settings	Potentially available	A local church with classrooms, rural church facilities, a rental guesthouse

Kinds of Training Materials Available in the Vernacular	Types of Potential Trainees Available	The Church's Partnership in Financial Areas
Not available	Full-time ministers, elders, and deacons, worship leaders, youth leaders, women's ministry leaders, home Bible study leaders, prayer group	Provide church facility, purchase training materials, self-sponsoring bivocational leaders
Not available	All local church leaders, women, youth, and children's ministry leaders	Rural churches can host a three- to five-day training, a group of churches jointly can host short-cycle trainings, regional office can sponsor trainees, trainees can afford to purchase training materials
Not available	Training of trainers, children, youth, and women ministry workers, evangelists, pastors, elders, and deacons	Some local churches can sponsor trainees, regional offices can sponsor trainees, trainees can afford to purchase training materials, initial subsidy for training of trainers needed
Not available	Church planters, local church leaders, pastors, evangelists, women ministry leaders	Some churches can sponsor their trainees, all churches can purchase training materials each worth 70–100 Ethiopian birr, formal training requires subsidy
Not available	Pastors, church planters, youth workers, children's ministry leaders, counselors, elders, and deacons	Churches can share limited amount of the training cost, formal training requires initial subsidy from outside
Not available	Training of trainers	Urban churches can afford to purchase materials, initial subsidy is needed to train rural church leaders

Participants	Medium of Instruction	Types of National Trainers Available	Types of Training Facilities Available
HBC leader from the North Shewa zone	Amharic in urban areas and Oromigna in rural areas	Potentially available	Local church facilities
HBC leader from Dire Dawa Administrative Council	Amharic and English for formal theological training, Amharic in urban areas and diverse ethnic languages in rural settings	Not available	A rental local church facility

Kinds of Training Materials Available in the Vernacular	Types of Potential Trainees Available	The Church's Partnership in Financial Areas
Not available	Training of trainers, local church leaders (150–210 of them from 30 congregations)	Some churches can afford to buy the training materials, a group of rural churches can jointly host a two- to three-day training
Not available	Existing leaders of four congregations and leaders of ministry departments in these churches	All four churches are still supported by the mother church to cover their operational costs. They cannot partner in financial areas

Bibliography

Adams, John Wesley, Roger D. Cotton, and Quentin McGhee. *Survey of the Old Testament*. Faith & Action. Springfield: Global University, 2003.

Adeyemo, Tokunboh. "Leadership." In *Africa Bible Commentary*, edited by Tokunboh Adeymo. Nairobi: WordAlive, 2006.

Alberto, Antonios. *The Apostolic Vicariate of Galla, a Capuchin Mission in Ethiopia (1846-1942)*. Addis Ababa: Capuchin Franciscan Institute of Philosophy and Theology, 1998.

Anderson, Allan. "The Fury and Wonder? Pentecostal-Charismatic Spirituality in Theological Education." *Pneuma: The Journal of the Society for Pentecostal Studies* 23, no. 2 (2001): 287–302.

Angrosino, Michael. *Doing Ethnographic and Observational Research*. London: SAGE, 2007.

Ararso, Solomon W. *Back to the Biblical Principles of Leadership*. N.p: N.p., 2013.

Arrington, French L., and Roger Stronstad, eds. *Life in the Spirit: New Testament Commentary*. Grand Rapids: Zondervan, 1999.

Babajide Cole, Victor. "Mark." In *Africa Bible Commentary*, edited by Tokunboh Adeymo. Nairobi: WordAlive, 2006.

Balisky, Paul. "Contemporary Theological Perspective." *Journal of Gudina Tumsa Theological Forum* 1 (2011): 39–58.

Banwell, Brian. "Christian Witness in Relation to Theological Education and Ministerial Formation." *International Review of Mission* 83, no. 328 (1994): 129–37.

Barbour, Rose. *Doing Focus Groups*. London: SAGE, 2007.

Barnett, Paul. *Jesus and the Rise of Early Christianity*. Downers Grove: InterVarsity Press, 1999.

Bellete, Getachew. *Agonies and Hallelujahs*. Addis Ababa: Ethiopian Kale Heywet Church, 2000.

Berhe, Axumawit, ed. "The Vision and Objective of Nazarene." *Nazarene* 2 (June 2014): 11.

Biza, Tenkir T. "Servant-Leadership Development: Assessing Leadership Development Programs and Strategies of Ethiopian Kale Heywet Church." MA thesis, Ethiopian Graduate School of Theology, 2011.

Buconyori, Elie A. *The Educational Task of the Church*. Kijabe: Kijabe Printing, 1993.

Camery-Hoggatt, Jerry. "Mark." In *Life in the Spirit: New Testament Commentary*, edited by French L Arrington and Roger Stronstad. Grand Rapids: Zondervan, 1999.

Central Statistical Agency of Ethiopia. *Population and Housing Census 2007*. Addis Ababa: CSA, 2007. CD-ROM.

Coleman, Robert E. *The Master Plan of Evangelism*. Grand Rapids: Revell, 1993.

Creswell, John W. *Educational Research*. 4th ed. Boston: Pearson, 2012.

Davies, Eddie. *The Training Managers: A Handbook*. New Delhi: Crest, 2003.

Degefa, Lemma. *Yehiwot Wuquir*. Addis Ababa: Rehoboth, 2006.

Draper, Jonathan A., and Edgar Ruddoch. "Ministerial Formation of Self-Supporting Minister in a Rural Environment." *Ministerial Formation* 40 (1987): 4–11.

Edwards, James R. *The Gospel According to Mark*. Pillar New Testament Commentary. Grand Rapids: Eerdmans, 2002.

Eims, Leroy. *Discipleship in Action*. Wheaton: NavPress, 1981.

Elliston, Edgar J. *Home Grown Leaders*. Pasadena: William Carey Library, 1992.

———. "Masai Leadership Development: An Emerging Process." *East Africa Journal of Theology* 2, no. 2 (1983): 20–31.

Ersulo, Wondaferaw A. "Bridging the Gap: Towards Developing Appropriate Leadership Approach for the Ethiopian Kale Heywet Church." Diss., Fuller Theological Seminary, 2009.

Ethiopian Hiwot Berhan Church. *Revised Constitution of the Ethiopian Hiwot Berhan Church*. Addis Ababa: Professional Printers, 2013.

Evans, Craig. "Mark." In *Eerdmans Commentary on the Bible*, eds James D. Dunn and John W. Rogerson. Grand Rapids: Eerdmans, 2003.

Fee, Gordon D. *Gospel and Spirit*. Peabody: Hendrickson, 1991.

Ferris, Robert E., ed. *Establishing Ministry Training*. Pasadena: William Carey Library, 1995.

Flick, Uwe, Ernst von Kardorff, and Ines Steinke, eds. *A Companion to Qualitative Research*. London: SAGE, 2004.

France, R. T. *The Gospel of Mark*. New International Greek New Testament Commentary. Grand Rapids: Eerdmans, 2002.

Fuliga, Jose B. "Problems in Theological Education: A Third World Perspective." *Asia Journal of Theology* 25, no. 2 (2011): 279–87.

Galvan, Jose L. *Writing Literature Reviews*. 4th ed. Glendale: Pyrczak, 2009.

G/Ammanuel, Mikre-Sellassie. *Church and Missions in Ethiopia during the Italian Occupation*. Addis Ababa: Artistic Printing Enterprise, 2014.

Gangel, Kenneth O. *Team Leadership in Christian Ministry*. Chicago: Moody, 1997.

Gatwa, Tharcisse. "Theological Education in Africa: What Prospects for Sharing Knowledge?" *Exchange* 32, no. 3 (2003): 194–213.

Girma, Yewbsefer. "Exploring the Participation of Women in Leadership in the Ethiopian Evangelical Churches: Ethiopian Kale Heywet Church, Addis Ababa Region." MA thesis, Ethiopian Graduate School of Theology, 2011.

Gooren, Henri. "The Pentecostalization of Religion and Society in Latin America." *Exchange* 39 (2010): 355–76.

Grudem, Wayne. *Systematic Theology*. Leicester: Inter-Varsity Press, 1994.

Guelich, Robert A. *Mark 1–8*. Dallas: Word, 1994.

Bakke, Johnny. "Models Of Leadership In Ethiopia: The Missionary Contribution." In *The Missionary Factor in Ethiopia*, edited by Getachew Haile, Aasulv Lande, and Samuel Rubenson, eds.. Frankfurt: Peter Lang, 1998.

Hatiya, Tesfahun, ed. "Yeethiopia Hiwot Berhan Bête Kristian Tinant." *Yehiwot Berhan* special ed. (July 2010): 18–23.

Hege, Nathan B. *Beyond Our Prayers*. Scottsdale: Herald, 1998.

Hiebert, Paul G. *Anthropological Reflections on Missiological Issues*. Grand Rapids: Baker, 1994.

Hodges, Melvin L. *A Guide to Church Planting and Development*. Chicago: Moody, 1973.

———. *The Indigenous Church*. Springfield: Gospel, 1953.

Horton, Stanley M., ed. *Systematic Theology*. Springfield: Logion, 1995.

Kalu, Ogbu U. "Elijah's Mantle: Ministerial Formation in Contemporary African Christianity." *International Review of Mission* 94, no. 373 (2005): 263–77.

Kassaye, Woube. "An Overview of Curriculum Development in Ethiopia: 1908–2005." *Ethiopian Journal of the Social Sciences and Humanities* 3, no. 1 (2005): 49–80.

Keck, Leaner E. *The New Interpreter's Bible*. Vol. 3. Nashville: Abingdon, 1995.

Keener, Craig S. *The IVP Bible Background Commentary: New Testament*. Downers Grove: InterVarsity Press, 1993.

Krallmann, Günter. *Mentoring for Mission*. Waynesboro: Gabriel, 2002.

Kuale, Steinar. *Doing Interviews*. London: SAGE, 2007.

Kunhiyop, Samuel Wade. "Witchcraft." In *Africa Bible Commentary*, edited by Tokunboh Adeymo. Nairobi: WordAlive, 2006.

Marshall, I. Howard, A. R. Millard, J. I. Packer, and D. J. Wiseman, eds. *New Bible Dictionary*. 3rd ed. Leicester: Inter-Varsity Press, 1996.

Mejia, Rodrigo. "Vocational and Professional Training for Religious: A Crucial Need in Africa Today." *Africa Ecclesial Review* , no. 34 (1992): 158–62.

Meyers, Paul C. "A Trinitarian Vision of Leadership in the Church." Diss., University of Dubuque Theological Seminary, 2008.
Nürnberger, Klaus. "Ministerial Training for the 21st Century: A South African Case Study." *Ministerial Formation* 98–99 (2002): 76–83.
Pentecostal Theological College. *Catalogue*. Addis Ababa: Pentecostal Theological College, n.d.
Pohor, Rubin. "Tribalism, Ethnicity and Race." In *Africa Bible Commentary*, edited by Tokunboh Adeymo. Nairobi: WordAlive, 2006.
Regggy-Mamo, Mae Alice. "Widow Inheritance." In *Africa Bible Commentary*, edited by Tokunboh Adeymo. Nairobi: WordAlive, 2006.
Sapsezian, Aharon. "Ministry with the Poor." *International Review of Mission* 66, no. 261 (Jan. 1977): 3–13.
Schultz, Samuel J. *The Old Testament Speaks*. San Francisco: Harper, 1990.
Scott, J. Julius, Jr. *Jewish Backgrounds of the New Testament*. Grand Rapids: Baker, 1995.
Sensing, Tim. *Qualitative Research*. Eugene: Wipf & Stock, 2011.
Shaw, Mark. *The Kingdom of God in Africa: A Short History of African Christianity*. Grand Rapids: Baker, 1996.
Short, Stephen S. "Mark." In *The International Bible Commentary*, edited by F. F. Bruce. Grand Rapids: Zondervan, 1986.
Simiyu, Oliver Kisaka. "The Need for Deliberate Christian Leadership Development in Africa: A Kenyan Perspective." *AICMAR Bulletin: An Evangelical Christian Journal of Contemporary Mission and Research in Africa* 1 (2002): 61–75.
Stein, Robert H. *Mark*. Baker Exegetical Commentary on the New Testament. Grand Rapids: Baker Academic, 2008.
Stronstad, Roger. *The Charismatic Theology of St. Luke*. Peabody: Hendrickson, 1984.
———. *Spirit, Scripture and Theology: A Pentecostal Perspective*. Baguio: Asia Pacific Theological Seminary, 1995; Grand Rapids: Zondervan, 1986.
Taylor, Vincent. *The Gospel According to St. Mark*. London: Macmillan, 1953.
Tennent, Timothy C. *Invitation to World Missions*. Grand Rapids: Kregel, 2010.
Tenney, Merrill C., ed. *The Zondervan Pictorial Bible Dictionary*. Grand Rapids: Zondervan, 1967.
Teshome, Daniel. *The Current (1987–2007) Reformation Movement within the Ethiopian Orthodox Tewahido Church*. Addis Ababa: Ethiopian Graduate School of Theology / Rehoboth, 2007.
Ullendorff, Edward. *The Ethiopians*. 2nd ed. London: Oxford University Press, 1960.
Walls, Andrew F. "World Christianity." *Transformation: An International Journal of Holistic Mission Studies* 28, no. 4 (2011): 235–40.

Walvoord, John F. *Jesus Christ Our Lord*. Chicago: Moody, 1969.

Wessel, Walter W. "Mark." In *The Expositor's Bible Commentary: Abridged Edition*, edited by Kenneth L. Barker and John R. Kholenberger III, 136–205. Grand Rapids: Zondervan, 1994.

Witherington, Ben, III. *The Gospel of Mark: A Socio-Rhetorical Commentary*. Grand Rapids: Eerdmans, 2001.

Woldesemait, Bekure. "Some Thoughts on Prospects for Achieving Food Security in Ethiopia: Resource and Policy Aspects." *Ethiopian Journal of the Social Sciences and Humanities* 3, no. 1 (2005): 21–47.

Wondimagegnehu, Aymro, and Joachim Motovu. *The Ethiopian Orthodox Church*. Addis Ababa: Berhanena Selam H.S.I., 1970.

Yilma, Daniel. "Evangelical Theological Education Impact Assessment in Evangelical Churches of Addis Ababa." MA thesis, Pan Africa Christian University, 2010.

Langham Literature, with its publishing work, is a ministry of Langham Partnership.

Langham Partnership is a global fellowship working in pursuit of the vision God entrusted to its founder John Stott –

> ***to facilitate the growth of the church in maturity and Christ-likeness through raising the standards of biblical preaching and teaching.***

Our vision is to see churches in the Majority World equipped for mission and growing to maturity in Christ through the ministry of pastors and leaders who believe, teach and live by the word of God.

Our mission is to strengthen the ministry of the word of God through:
- nurturing national movements for biblical preaching
- fostering the creation and distribution of evangelical literature
- enhancing evangelical theological education

especially in countries where churches are under-resourced.

Our ministry

Langham Preaching partners with national leaders to nurture indigenous biblical preaching movements for pastors and lay preachers all around the world. With the support of a team of trainers from many countries, a multi-level programme of seminars provides practical training, and is followed by a programme for training local facilitators. Local preachers' groups and national and regional networks ensure continuity and ongoing development, seeking to build vigorous movements committed to Bible exposition.

Langham Literature provides Majority World preachers, scholars and seminary libraries with evangelical books and electronic resources through publishing and distribution, grants and discounts. The programme also fosters the creation of indigenous evangelical books in many languages, through writer's grants, strengthening local evangelical publishing houses, and investment in major regional literature projects, such as one volume Bible commentaries like the Africa Bible Commentary and the South Asia Bible Commentary.

Langham Scholars provides financial support for evangelical doctoral students from the Majority World so that, when they return home, they may train pastors and other Christian leaders with sound, biblical and theological teaching. This programme equips those who equip others. Langham Scholars also works in partnership with Majority World seminaries in strengthening evangelical theological education. A growing number of Langham Scholars study in high quality doctoral programmes in the Majority World itself. As well as teaching the next generation of pastors, graduated Langham Scholars exercise significant influence through their writing and leadership.

To learn more about Langham Partnership and the work we do visit langham.org

www.ingramcontent.com/pod-product-compliance
Lightning Source LLC
Chambersburg PA
CBHW070613170426
43200CB00012B/2681